Family Circle® ABZ's of Cooking

Edited by Lucy Wing with
The Family Circle Food Department

Volume 1

Introduction

Family Circle's *ABZ's of Cooking* is a unique 12-volume encyclopedia series—packed with the information every kitchen manager wants and needs, and organized alphabetically so that each cooking subject is easily found.

Family Circle is the world's leading women's service magazine. Millions of Americans have grown up with our recipes, and now serve them to their own families. Our readers look to us for new ideas and traditional favorites; for recipes they enjoy making, and take pride in serving.

The magazine's distinguished food department, along with food expert Lucy Wing, have pulled together hundreds of Family Circle's greatest recipes for this series. Every one has been updated for the 80's. Each has been carefully written and triple-tested to reflect today's tastes, with the newest equipment and techniques. Definitions of foods and cooking terms have been stated, as well as buying, storage and preparation guidelines.

Each volume has recipes for appetizers, salads, main dishes, vegetables, and desserts so that you can make complete meals from just one volume. Beautiful color photographs of finished dishes appear throughout. All-in-all, this series adds up to one of the most comprehensive and contemporary cooking libraries available.

This first volume contains all the information and recipes you'll ever need for the best in home-cooking—from Abalone through Beverages.

Contents

Cover photo
Apple-Almond Tart, page 25

ISBN 0-8249-9001-3 b

Printed and bound in the United States of America.
Published by Ideals Publishing Corporation
11315 Watertown Plank Road
Milwaukee, WI 53226

Family Circle Staff
Project Editor Lucy Wing
Food Editor Jean Hewitt
Senior Associate Food Editor Jane O'Keefe
Art Director Joseph Taveroni
Copy Editors Karen Saks, Susan Tierney
Project Management Annabelle Arenz, John Jaxheimer

Ideals Publishing Staff
Project Editor Julie Hogan
Food Stylist Susan Noland
Photographer Gerald Koser
Project Management James Kuse, Marybeth Owens

Photographs by: Avedis, Paul Christensen, Richard Jeffery, Allen Lieberman, Bill McGinn, Rudy Muller, George Nordhausen, Gordon E. Smith, Bob Stoller, Rene Velez

ABALONE A large univalve (single-shell) mollusk or shellfish. The edible portion is the central muscle which resembles a large sea scallop. This muscle enables the abalone to cling to the rocks.

There are many species found along the Pacific coastal areas of the United States and Mexico, and along the Asian coast.

A great delicacy, abalone is highly prized in Oriental cooking. The mother-of-pearl shell lining is used for jewelry, buttons, and inlaid wood carvings.

Fresh abalone must be cut into strips or slices and pounded to tenderize before cooking. Avoid overcooking to keep it from becoming tough and rubbery.

ACORN SQUASH This variety of hard-skinned winter squash is available in markets all year, but supplies are best in the fall. Acorn squash is distinguished by its oval or round ribbed-shape and inedible dark green rind. The flesh is yellow-orange with a slightly sweet, nutty taste. Store in a cool dry place.

To Prepare: Wash; cut in half lengthwise. Scrape out seeds. Cut small slice off bottom of each half so it will stand level when served.

To Bake: Place squash halves, cut sides down, in shallow baking pan. Add ½ inch water. Bake in a moderate oven (375°) for 30 minutes. Turn cut sides up. Sprinkle with salt, pepper and ground cinnamon or nutmeg. Spread ½ tablespoon butter or margarine on cut edges. Add brown sugar, maple syrup, honey or chopped nuts to cavity if you wish. Bake 10 minutes more or until squash is tender.

To Microwave: For 2 to 4 squash halves, place in square dish, cut sides down. Cover with plastic wrap or wax paper. Microwave on high power for 8 minutes. Turn cut sides up; brush with butter. Microwave 5 to 8 minutes more. Let stand 5 minutes.

ACORN SQUASH WITH PEAS

Makes 8 servings.

- **4 medium-size acorn squash**
- **½ cup (1 stick) of butter or margarine**
- **¼ teaspoon pepper**
- **½ teaspoon onion salt**
- **2 packages (10 ounces each) frozen peas in butter sauce**

1. Scrub squash well; halve; scrape out seeds. Cut lengthwise into 1-inch-wide slices. Cook in boiling salted water just until tender, about 15 minutes. Drain. Add butter, pepper and salt. Cover; keep warm.
2. Cook peas following label directions.
3. Spoon both vegetables into heated serving dish.

LAMB-STUFFED ACORN SQUASH

Bake at 375° for 1 hour.
Makes 4 servings.

- **2 small acorn squash (2 pounds), halved and seeded**
- **1 pound ground lamb**
- **1 medium-size onion, chopped (½ cup)**
- **2 tablespoons vegetable oil**
- **1 teaspoon mint flakes, crumbled**
- **¼ teaspoon ground cinnamon**
- **¾ teaspoon salt**
- **¼ teaspoon pepper**
- **2 tablespoons chopped parsley**
- **2 tablespoons dried currants**
- **2 teaspoons vinegar**
- **1 cup frozen mixed vegetables**
- **1 can (8 ounces) tomato sauce**
- **2 tablespoons pine nuts**

1. Place squash, cut sides down, in shallow baking pan; add ½ inch water.
2. Bake in a moderate oven (375°) for 30 minutes; turn cut sides up; bake 10 more minutes.
3. Prepare filling while squash bakes. Sauté lamb and onion in oil in large skillet; stir in remaining ingredients. Cook over low heat 5 minutes to blend flavors.
4. Mound ½ cup filling in each squash half. (Any extra filling may be wrapped in a foil packet and baked along with squash or frozen.)
5. Bake squash 20 minutes longer or just until heated through.

ALLSPICE Despite its name, allspice is only one spice. Its aroma and flavor does resemble several spices like cinnamon, cloves and nutmeg. Most allspice comes from Jamaica. The reddish-brown, ¼-inch berries are dried and either ground or sold as whole berries. The most common uses are in pickles, relishes, cakes, cookies and stewed fruit.

ALMONDS Botanically classified a fruit, the almond is the ancestor of other stone fruit such as nectarines, plums, apricots and peaches. The almond has a tough grey-green hull which resembles a small, long peach. At maturity, the hull opens to reveal the almond shell which encloses the nut.

Almonds grew in ancient China and the Middle East, and later, in Spain and Italy. In the mid-1700's, almonds were brought to California via Mexico by Franciscan Padres. Today, California supplies most of the world's almonds.

Almonds are sold in numerous forms: *Unshelled* in the hard, pale tan-colored shell; *whole natural,* in which the shells are removed; *whole blanched* have the shells and skins removed; *sliced natural* are thinly sliced lengthwise; *sliced blanched* are blanched and thinly sliced lengthwise; *blanched slivered* are blanched, halved and then cut lengthwise into strips; *chopped natural* are natural almonds chopped and ready to use in recipes. Almonds are also *roasted whole, blanched* or *natural, flavored* for snacking, *roasted slivered* or *diced.* Store almonds in an airtight container in refrigerator or freezer.

Almond Tidbits: To oven roast, spread nuts in a shallow pan coated with butter or oil. Bake in a moderate oven (350°) 10 minutes or until golden, shaking pan occasionally. To skillet roast, heat almonds in butter or oil until nuts are golden, shaking pan occasionally. To toast almonds in oven or skillet, follow the same procedures but omit fat. To blanch almonds, put whole shelled nuts in saucepan; cover with water. Heat to boiling; drain; add cold water. Drain and press each nut between fingers to slip skin off. See also **NUTS**.

Nutrition: Almonds are rich in magnesium and phosphorus. Riboflavin is present in good quantity. One ounce, about 20-25 nuts, has 170 calories.

Almond Math

1 pound in shells = 1¾ cups shelled
1 pound shelled = 2⅔ cups
1 cup sliced = 3¼ ounces
1 cup slivered = 4½ ounces

AMBROSIA A dessert of assorted sweet fruit and shredded coconut. It can also be a sweet beverage. In Greek mythology, ambrosia was the food of the gods.

AMBROSIA

Makes about 12 servings.

2 large pineapples
OR: 3 cans (20 ounces each) pineapple chunks in juice
12 large oranges
3 cups grated fresh coconut
OR: 2 cans (4 ounces each) shredded coconut

1. Pare and core the fresh pineapple; cut the fruit into chunks into a large bowl, saving as much juice as possible. (For canned pineapple, use all the juice.)
2. Remove rind from oranges with a sharp knife, holding fruit over bowl to catch juice. Slice oranges, removing any seeds.
3. Layer pineapple, part of the coconut and oranges in a serving bowl. Sprinkle top with remaining coconut. Cover; chill at least 4 hours before serving.

•●•

AMERICAN REGIONAL FOOD Although we owe much of our food heritage to other cultures, our own contributions are rich and varied. Here are some regional specialties.

New England

Colonial women used local foodstuffs like corn, turkey and beans to create dishes that have become distinct American classics.

NEW ENGLAND BOILED DINNER

Colonists preserved meat by pickling it in brine or drying it. Pickled meat resulted in corned beef. Dried meat was called jerky. Boiled dinners were one-pot colonial meals created for those busy days.

Makes 10 servings.

1 corned beef brisket (about 4 pounds)
3 large yellow turnips, pared and cut into ½-inch slices
1 pound carrots, pared and cut into chunks
6 medium-size potatoes, pared and halved
1 bunch beets without tops
2 medium-size heads of cabbage, each cut into 6 wedges
¼ cup (½ stick) butter or margarine, melted
Chopped parsley
Creamy Horseradish Sauce *(recipe follows)*

1. Simmer corned beef in water to cover in a large kettle for 2 hours. Add the turnips; cook 30 minutes. Add the carrots and potatoes; cook 30 minutes longer or until meat and vegetables are tender.
2. About 1 hour before meat is done, cook beets in water in a large saucepan until tender; skin; keep warm.
3. Start cooking cabbage in a large kettle of water, about 30 minutes before meat is done.
4. Drain meat; arrange on a large warm platter. Spoon hot vegetables around meat; pour melted butter over vegetables; sprinkle with parsley. Serve with Creamy Horseradish Sauce or mustard.

CREAMY HORSERADISH SAUCE

Makes 1¼ cups.

½ cup heavy cream
3 tablespoons prepared horseradish
1 teaspoon sugar
¼ teaspoon salt
⅛ teaspoon pepper

Beat cream in a small bowl with electric mixer until soft peaks form. Fold in horseradish, sugar, salt and pepper. Refrigerate.

Pictured opposite: New England Boiled Dinner with Creamy Horseradish Sauce, page 5

STEAMED BOSTON BROWN BREAD

A true New England contribution to our cooking. Its favorite companion is baked beans.

Steam 3 hours.
Bake at 325° for 10 minutes.
Makes two 1-pound loaves.

1 cup cornmeal
1 cup whole-wheat or graham flour
1 cup rye flour
1 teaspoon salt
1 teaspoon baking soda
1 tablespoon water
½ cup molasses
2 tablespoons vinegar or lemon juice
Milk
1 cup raisins
2 tablespoons all-purpose flour

1. Combine cornmeal, whole-wheat flour, rye flour and salt in a large mixing bowl.
2. Stir baking soda into water in a medium-size bowl; add molasses.
3. Put vinegar in a 2-cup measure. Add milk to make 2 cups. Combine with molasses mixture. Stir liquids into dry ingredients until well mixed.
4. Combine raisins and flour in a small bowl; add to batter.
5. Pour batter into two greased 1-quart molds or clean coffee cans. Cover tightly with a double-thickness of aluminum foil.
6. Place molds on rack in kettle. Add boiling water to halfway up sides of molds. Cover kettle. Steam 3 hours, adding more boiling water as necessary to keep proper level. Unmold loaves; place on cookie sheet.
7. Bake in a slow oven (325°) for 10 minutes to dry. Cool loaves.
8. To serve: Purists say to slice bread with string, never with a knife.

NEW ENGLAND BAKED BEANS

Get out your best bean pot and enjoy this stick-to-the-ribs classic.

Bake at 275° for 5 hours.
Makes 6 servings.

1 pound dried navy or pea beans
6 cups water
½ pound salt pork
1 large onion, chopped (1 cup)
⅔ cup maple syrup
3 tablespoons dark molasses
2 tablespoons prepared mustard
1 teaspoon salt

1. Pick over and wash beans. Soak overnight in cold water to cover in a large bowl. Or, to quick soak, bring beans and water to boiling in large kettle; boil 2 minutes, remove from heat; let stand 1 hour.
2. Drain beans; combine with the 6 cups water in a large kettle or Dutch oven. Bring to boiling; lower heat; simmer 45 minutes or until beans are firm-tender.
3. Drain beans, reserving water. Slash salt pork in several places, cutting almost but not quite through. Combine beans and pork with onion in a 2-quart bean pot or deep baking dish.
4. Stir maple syrup, molasses, mustard and salt in a small bowl until blended; stir gently into bean mixture.
5. Pour enough reserved bean water to fill the bean pot and just cover the beans; reserve any remaining water.
6. Bake, covered, in a very slow oven (275°) for 3 hours. Uncover; bake 2 hours longer. Stir beans occasionally during baking and add more reserved water whenever needed.

CHOCOLATE CHIP COOKIES

In 1940, the owner of a Massachusetts restaurant, the Toll House, dropped chopped chocolate pieces into her cookie dough when she ran out of raisins—and thus, the birth of the chocolate chip cookie! Today there are hundreds of variations; ours includes nuts as well as chocolate.

Bake at 350° for 8 minutes.
Makes about 4 dozen cookies.

1¾ cups *sifted* all-purpose flour
½ teaspoon baking soda
¼ teaspoon salt
¾ cup (1½ sticks) butter or margarine, softened
½ cup granulated sugar
¼ cup firmly packed light or dark brown sugar
1 egg
1 teaspoon vanilla
1 cup chopped walnuts or pecans
1 package (6 ounces) semi-sweet chocolate pieces

1. Sift flour, baking soda and salt onto wax paper.
2. Beat butter, granulated and brown sugars, egg and vanilla in a large bowl with electric mixer until fluffy. Preheat oven to 350°.
3. Stir in flour mixture by hand until mixed. Stir in nuts and chocolate.
4. Drop dough by rounded teaspoonful, 1 inch apart, onto greased cookie sheets.
5. Bake in a preheated moderate oven (350°) for 8 minutes or until cookies are golden brown. Remove from cookie sheets; cool on wire racks. When thoroughly cool, store in covered containers.

Note: For larger cookies, drop dough by rounded tablespoonsful onto greased cookie sheets. Increase baking time to 10 to 12 minutes.

Pennsylvania Dutch

The Pennsylvania Dutch are not Dutch at all. The word "Dutch" is a corruption of "Deutsch" meaning German. Southeastern Pennsylvania is home to these European emigrants, who are known for their gracious hospitality and hearty foods.

RED BEET EGGS

Makes 10 servings.

10 hard-cooked eggs, peeled
2 cans (16 ounces each) sliced beets with juice
1 cup water
½ cup cider or distilled white vinegar
½ teaspoon salt
¼ teaspoon pepper
Curly endive

1. Combine eggs, beets, water, vinegar, salt and pepper in a large bowl. Cover: Refrigerate at least 8 hours or overnight.
2. To serve: Drain eggs and beets. Line a serving plate with endive. Cut eggs in half; arrange on plate with sliced beets. Serve immediately.

CHICKEN CORN SOUP

Makes about 3 quarts.

- **1 stewing chicken, cut up (about 5 pounds)**
- **8 cups water**
- **2 tablespoons salt**
- **10 whole peppercorns**
- **1 bay leaf**
- **2 small onions, peeled**
- **2 celery tops**
- **2 packages (10 ounces each) frozen whole-kernel corn**
- **⅛ teaspoon crumbled saffron threads**
- **2 tablespoons chopped fresh parsley**

1. Combine chicken, water, salt, peppercorns, bay leaf, onions and celery tops in a large kettle. Bring slowly to boiling; lower heat. Simmer slowly for 2 to 2½ hours or until meat is very tender. Remove meat from the broth.
2. Strain broth through cheesecloth into large bowl. When cool enough to handle, remove skin and bones from chicken; cut meat into bite-size pieces. Skim as much fat as possible from broth or refrigerate until fat solidifies.
3. To serve: Return chicken to broth; bring to boiling. Add corn and saffron; simmer 10 minutes or until corn is tender. Taste and add more salt and pepper if necessary. Stir in parsley.

SHOOFLY PIE

Bake at 350° for 30 minutes.
Makes one 9-inch pie.

- **1½ cups *sifted* all-purpose flour**
- **1 cup firmly packed light or dark brown sugar**
- **½ cup (1 stick) butter or margarine**
- **¼ teaspoon salt**
- **½ teaspoon baking soda**
- **⅔ cup hot water**
- **⅔ cup dark molasses**
- **1 unbaked 9-inch pastry shell**

1. Combine the flour, brown sugar, butter or margarine and salt and rub the mixture between the hands to form crumbs. Preheat oven to 350°.
2. Dissolve the baking soda in the water and combine with molasses. Pour into pastry shell. Sprinkle evenly with crumbs.
3. Bake in a preheated moderate oven (350°) for 30 to 40 minutes or until filling is set. Cool on wire rack.

CHOW CHOW

Makes about 3 quarts.

- **2 cups coarsely chopped celery**
- **2 cups sliced carrots**
- **2 cups coarsely chopped red and green peppers**
- **2 cups cauliflowerettes (½ head)**
- **2 cups small white onions, peeled**
- **1 package (9 ounces) frozen cut green beans**
- **1 package (10 ounces) frozen lima beans**
- **1 can (16 ounces) yellow wax beans, drained**
- **2 jars (8 ounces each) sweet gherkins**
- **3 cups sugar**
- **2 cups cider vinegar**
- **1 cup water**
- **1½ tablespoons mustard seeds**
- **1 tablespoon celery seeds**
- **½ teaspoon turmeric**

1. Cook each vegetable except yellow wax beans separately in boiling salted water until just tender but still firm. Drain. Combine in a large bowl. Add canned beans. Drain juice from gherkins into bowl; chop gherkins finely and add to bowl.
2. Combine sugar, vinegar, water, mustard seeds, celery seeds and turmeric in large kettle. Bring to boiling, stirring constantly until sugar dissolves. Add vegetable mixture. After mixture comes to boiling again, boil 5 minutes, stirring often.
3. Ladle into hot, sterilized jars to within ¼ inch from top. Seal, following manufacturer's directions; process in hot water bath 15 minutes. Let jars cool. Label, date and store in a cool place.

Southern

Southern cooking means good home cooking. Southern cooks popularized chicken by rolling it in flour and frying it in fat, not to mention using pecans, a native nut, as filling for a pie.

SOUTHERN CHESS PIE

Nobody really knows the origin of this pie, but it's probably a variation of the traditional English chess pie.

Bake at 375° for 45 minutes.
Makes one 7½-inch pie.

- **1 unbaked 7½-inch* pastry shell**
- **½ cup (1 stick) butter or margarine**
- **1½ cups sugar**
- **3 eggs**
- **1 tablespoon white vinegar**
- **1 teaspoon vanilla**

1. Prepare pastry shell; chill. Heat butter and sugar in a small saucepan until butter is melted (do not boil); cool slightly. Preheat oven to 375°.
2. Beat eggs in a large bowl until frothy. Add vinegar, vanilla and butter-sugar mixture; mix well. Pour mixture into unbaked shell.
3. Bake in a preheated moderate oven (375°) for about 45 minutes or until center is almost set but still soft. Cool thoroughly on wire rack before cutting.

**Oven-proof glass pie plates now sold in stores are marked "7½ inches." Older pie plates marked "8 inches" can also be used.*

CORN BREAD

Bake at 425° for 20 minutes.
Makes 9 servings.

- **1 cup yellow cornmeal**
- **1 cup *sifted* all-purpose flour**
- **2 teaspoons sugar**
- **½ teaspoon salt**
- **4 teaspoons baking powder**
- **1 egg, lightly beaten**
- **1 cup milk**
- **¼ cup shortening, butter or margarine, melted**

1. Sift the cornmeal, flour, sugar, salt and baking powder into a bowl. Stir in the egg, milk and melted shortening until the dry ingredients are just moistened. Preheat oven to 450°.
2. Heat a lightly greased 8-inch square baking pan on top of the stove. Spoon in the corn mixture.
3. Bake in a preheated hot oven (425°) for 20 to 25 minutes or until done. Cut into squares to serve.

American Regional

VIRGINIA PECAN PIE

Bake at 350° for 45 minutes.
Makes one 9-inch pie.

- **½ package piecrust mix**
- **4 eggs**
- **1 cup sugar**
- **¼ cup all-purpose flour**
- **½ teaspoon salt**
- **1½ cups dark corn syrup**
- **1 teaspoon vanilla**
- **1 cup pecan halves**

1. Prepare piecrust mix for a single crust, following label directions. Roll out to a 13-inch round on a lightly floured board; fit into a 9-inch pie plate. Trim overhang to 1 inch; turn under, flush with rim; flute to make a stand-up edge. Preheat oven to 350°.
2. Beat eggs slightly in a medium-size bowl. Stir in sugar, flour, salt, corn syrup and vanilla. Pour into prepared shell; arrange pecan halves in pattern on top. Or, chop pecans coarsely; sprinkle into shell before adding filling.
3. Bake in a preheated moderate oven (350°) for 45 minutes or until center is almost set but still soft. (Do not overbake, for filling will set as it cools.) Cool on wire rack. Serve with whipped cream, if you wish.

FRIED CHICKEN WITH CREAM GRAVY

Fried chicken is a purely American dish; European versions were usually cooked and served in a sauce. At first, fried chicken was a seasonal treat, since there was no refrigeration and a new crop of chickens was only started in spring. Today, fried chicken is served hot or cold, at any time of the year. You're sure to enjoy this crunchy-crusted recipe.

Makes 4 servings.

- **1 broiler-fryer (about 3 pounds), cut up**
- **1 cup all-purpose flour**
- **2 teaspoons salt**
- **¾ teaspoon pepper**
- **½ teaspoon poultry seasoning**
- **½ cup light cream or half-and-half**
- **Vegetable oil**
- **Cream Gravy *(recipe follows)***

1. Wash and dry chicken pieces; shake in a bag with flour, salt, pepper and poultry seasoning. Dip coated pieces in cream in pie plate; then dip in remaining flour mixture to coat evenly.
2. Pour enough oil into large skillet to make a depth of 1 inch. Heat over moderate heat to 375° on deep-fat frying thermometer. Add chicken, skin side down. When underside of chicken starts to brown, lower heat and partially cover skillet with lid.
3. Turn chicken pieces after 15 minutes. Continue cooking second side, uncovered, until browned and chicken is tender, 10 minutes longer. Drain on paper toweling. Keep warm. Serve with Cream Gravy, if you wish.

Cream Gravy: Pour off fat from skillet, leaving brown bits; return 2 tablespoons fat to pan. Stir in 2 tablespoons flour; heat until light brown. Remove from heat; gradually stir in 1 cup light cream. Return to heat; cook, stirring constantly, until thickened and bubbly. If too thick, add more cream or milk. Taste and add salt and pepper as needed. Makes about 1¼ cups.

Midwest

The heartland of the United States is a vast area known for its production of beef, pork, wheat, corn and wild rice.

IOWA CORN PUDDING

Among the many foods that were new to the early settlers, corn was one of the most abundant and adaptable. With the help of the Indians, the Colonists soon learned how to grind corn into meal (for use in such staples as corncakes) and how to make hominy. Soon they learned to prepare many different corn dishes, including baked corn pudding.

Bake at 275° for 40 minutes.
Makes 4 servings.

- **2 teaspoons butter**
- **3 tablespoons chopped green pepper**
- **2 tablespoons chopped onion**
- **3 eggs**
- **1 cup milk**
- **2 teaspoons sugar**
- **1 teaspoon flour**
- **1 teaspoon salt**
- **⅛ teaspoon pepper**
- **1 package (10 ounces) frozen whole-kernel corn, thawed and drained**

1. Melt butter in small skillet; sauté green pepper and onion until tender, about 3 minutes. Remove from heat.
2. Beat eggs in medium-size bowl; stir in milk. Mix sugar, flour, salt and pepper in small cup; stir into egg-milk mixture. Add cooked pepper and onion and the corn. Turn into a buttered 4- to 6-cup shallow baking dish or 9-inch pie plate.
3. Bake in a slow oven (275°) for 40 minutes or until softly-set.

ALL-AMERICAN BURGERS

The first broiled hamburgers were served in 1904 at the St. Louis Exposition; they've been America's #1 favorite ever since. Try this home-style version of the "big stacked" burger.

Makes 6 burgers.

- **½ cup mayonnaise or salad dressing**
- **¼ cup chili sauce**
- **¼ cup sweet pickle relish**
- **1½ pounds ground round or chuck**
- **1 teaspoon salt**
- **⅛ teaspoon pepper**
- **2 tablespoons butter or margarine**
- **6 crisp, washed lettuce leaves**
- **6 hamburger rolls, halved**
- **6 tomato slices**
- **6 slices process American cheese**
- **6 thin slices sweet Bermuda onion**

1. Combine mayonnaise, chili sauce and sweet pickle relish in a small bowl; mix until well blended; cover. Refrigerate sauce until ready to use.
2. Mix beef lightly with salt and pepper; shape into 6 patties.
3. Melt butter in a large skillet. Panfry hamburgers over medium heat 2 minutes on each side, or until done as you like them.
4. To assemble: Put lettuce leaf on bottom half of roll; top with hamburger, a spoonful of the sauce, a tomato slice, cheese slice, more sauce and onion slice; top with remaining half of roll.

Pictured opposite: Virginia Pecan Pie, page 8

DEVIL'S FOOD CAKE

So wickedly delicious, someone called it "the devil's own food." This kind of ultra-chocolatey cake has pleased generations of Americans.

Bake at 350° for 35 minutes.
Makes one 9-inch cake.

3 squares unsweetened chocolate
2¼ cups *sifted* cake flour
2 teaspoons baking soda
½ teaspoon salt
½ cup (1 stick) butter or margarine
1¾ cups firmly packed light brown sugar
3 large eggs
2 teaspoons vanilla
1 container (8 ounces) dairy sour cream
1 cup boiling water
Fluffy 7-Minute Frosting *(recipe follows)*
1 square unsweetened chocolate
1 tablespoon butter or margarine

1. Melt chocolate in small bowl over hot, not boiling, water; cool.
2. Grease and flour two 9×1½-inch layer cake pans or one 13×9×2-inch baking pan; tap out excess flour.
3. Sift flour, baking soda and salt onto wax paper.
4. Beat butter until soft in large bowl. Add brown sugar and eggs; beat with electric mixer at high speed until light and fluffy, 5 minutes. Beat in vanilla and cooled melted chocolate. Preheat oven to 350°.
5. Stir in dry ingredients with spoon alternately with sour cream after each addition until batter is smooth. Stir in boiling water. (Batter will be thin.) Pour at once into prepared pans.
6. Bake in a preheated moderate oven (350°) for 35 minutes or until centers spring back when lightly pressed with fingertip.
7. Cool cake in pans on wire rack 10 minutes; loosen around edges with a small knife or spatula; turn out onto wire racks; cool completely. If using 13×9×2-inch pan, split cooled cake to make 2 layers.
8. Make Fluffy 7-Minute Frosting. Place one cake layer on a serving plate; spread with about ¼ of the frosting; place second layer over. Gently brush off loose crumbs. Frost sides and top, swirling frosting with spatula.
9. Melt chocolate square with the butter in a cup over hot water; stir until smooth. Drizzle over top of cake, letting mixture drip down side.

FLUFFY 7-MINUTE FROSTING

Makes enough to fill and frost two 8- or 9-inch cake layers or one 13×9×2-inch cake.

1½ cups sugar
¼ cup water
2 egg whites
2 tablespoons light corn syrup
¼ teaspoon salt
1 teaspoon vanilla

1. Combine sugar, water, egg whites, corn syrup and salt in top of double boiler; beat mixture until well blended.
2. Place over simmering water; cook, beating constantly at high speed with electric hand mixer or rotary beater about 7 minutes, or until mixture triples in volume and holds firm peaks. Remove from heat; beat in vanilla. Spread on cooled cake while still warm.

HERB-STUFFED PORK CHOPS

Bake at 350° for 1 hour.
Makes 4 servings.

½ pound medium-size mushrooms
⅓ cup chopped onion
⅓ cup chopped celery
½ cup (1 stick) butter or margarine
1 cup packaged bread crumbs
¼ teaspoon ground sage
½ cup chopped fresh parsley
½ cup dried apricots
4 double-ribbed center loin pork chops with pockets
½ teaspoon salt
¼ teaspoon pepper
1 cup dry white wine
Sweet-Sour Red Cabbage *(recipe follows)*

1. Reserve 4 mushrooms for garnish; thinly slice remainder. Sauté sliced mushrooms, onion and celery in ¼ cup of the butter in a large flameproof baking dish or skillet with an ovenproof handle until tender, about 3 minutes. Add bread crumbs, sage and parsley.
2. Reserve 4 apricots; chop remainder; add to skillet mixture. Sprinkle pork chops inside and out with salt and pepper. Stuff pork chop pockets loosely with mixture. Secure openings with wooden picks. Wipe out dish.
3. Brown chops on both sides in remaining ¼ cup butter in same ovenproof dish. Pour wine around chops; cover dish.
4. Bake in a moderate oven (350°) for 1 hour or until chops are tender. Garnish with reserved mushrooms and apricots, and add a few crisp celery tops for color. Serve with Sweet-Sour Red Cabbage.

Sweet-Sour Red Cabbage: Sauté 1 small chopped onion in 3 tablespoons butter in a Dutch oven or large skillet until tender, about 3 minutes. Shred 1 medium-size head red cabbage; add to pan with ½ cup orange juice and ½ teaspoon salt. Cover; simmer 10 minutes. Stir in 1 cup cranberries, ¼ cup water and ½ cup sugar; re-cover; simmer 5 minutes longer. Combine 2 teaspoons cornstarch with 3 tablespoons vinegar; add to pan; cook and stir until thickened.

WILD RICE

Makes about 10 servings.

2 cups wild rice
Boiling water
3 cans (13¾ ounces each) chicken broth
¾ cup water
2 tablespoons butter

Wash rice in colander under cold running water. Transfer to a large saucepan or Dutch oven. Cover with boiling water; let cool to lukewarm. Drain and return to saucepan. Repeat soaking with boiling water and draining twice more. Return drained rice to saucepan. Add chicken broth and water. Cover; bring to boiling. Uncover; lower heat, simmer about 30 minutes or until just tender and liquid is almost evaporated. Drain; stir in butter until melted.

Southwest

This region is known for a wide variety of foods, but the Tex-Mex dishes—tacos, burritos and enchiladas—are among the most notable. Tex-Mex dishes make full use of such New World foods as tomatoes, corn, beans and chilies.

CHEESE CRISP

This is a quick and irresistible appetizer or snack. Traditionally, it is served whole at the table and everyone breaks off a piece but it may be precut into wedges like pizza.

Makes about 8 servings.

1 large flour tortilla (about 14-inches in diameter)
1 tablespoon butter or margarine, softened
½ cup shredded longhorn or mild Cheddar cheese

Spread tortilla with butter or margarine. Heat on hot griddle or very large skillet until crisp and firm. Sprinkle with cheese; bake just until cheese melts. Garnish with strips of green chile, if you wish.

FRUIT EMPANADAS

These crisp, deep-fried turnovers, made here as a dessert, can also be filled with a meat mixture to serve as appetizers.

Makes 16 empanadas.

1½ cups *unsifted* all-purpose flour
1 teaspoon baking powder
½ teaspoon salt
⅓ cup lard or vegetable shortening
About ⅓ cup milk
Pineapple Filling *(recipe follows)*
Vegetable oil for frying

1. Mix flour, baking powder and salt in bowl. Cut in lard with pastry blender or two knives until mixture resembles cornmeal. Sprinkle with milk; mix with fork until dough clings together. (Add a little more milk, if necessary.)
2. Gather dough into a ball and knead about 10 times until smooth. Roll dough on lightly floured surface to ⅛-inch thickness. Cut into 4-inch circles with floured cookie cutter. Fill each with about 1 tablespoon filling; moisten edge with water. Fold in half and press edges to seal. Press edge with tip of fork. Reroll trimmings; cut and fill.
3. Heat ½ to 1 inch oil in a small skillet to 370°. Lower 4 or 5 empanadas in hot oil. Fry 2 minutes, turning once, until golden brown. Drain on paper toweling. Serve warm or cold. Dust with 10X (confectioners') sugar, if you wish.

PINEAPPLE FILLING

Makes about 1 cup.

1 can (8 ounces) crushed pineapple in pineapple juice
2 tablespoons sugar
1 tablespoon cornstarch
1½ teaspoons butter or margarine
1 teaspoon grated lemon rind

Combine pineapple, sugar, cornstarch, butter and lemon rind in small saucepan. Cook over medium heat until mixture is bubbly thick. Cool to room temperature.

CHIMICHANGAS

A chimichanga is a burrito or rolled, stuffed flour tortilla that has been fried to a golden crispness. The frying changes the flavor and texture of the tortilla. Chimichangas can be made with any type filling, such as chili con carne, refried beans or cheese.

Makes 8 servings.

1½ pounds beef chuck or round, cut into 1½-inch pieces
1½ pounds boneless pork shoulder, cut into 2-inch chunks
4 cups water
2 tablespoons lard or vegetable shortening
1 large onion, chopped (1 cup)
¾ to 1 cup canned diced, mild green chilies (about two 4-ounce cans)
1 clove garlic, minced
2 tablespoons flour
2 teaspoons salt
½ teaspoon ground cumin
8 large flour tortillas
Vegetable oil for frying
Green Chile Salsa *(recipe follows)*

1. Heat beef, pork and water to boiling in a large kettle; lower heat; cover. Simmer until meat is fork tender, about 1½ hours. Drain meat and reserve 1 cup broth. Shred meat when cool enough to handle.
2. Heat lard in a large saucepan. Add onion, ¾ cup chilies and garlic; sauté 1 minute. Add flour, salt and cumin; cook 1 minute. Stir in reserved broth and shredded meat; cook until mixture is moist but quite thick. (Add more chilies if you like it hotter.) Keep meat mixture warm.
3. Heat 1 tortilla on a large griddle or very large skillet over low heat until soft and pliable. Spread about ¾ cup meat mixture over the lower third of the tortilla in a band about 4 inches long and 1 inch wide. Work quickly so that tortilla does not get crisp. Fold the bottom edge of the tortilla up over filling to cover it almost completely. Then fold the two sides in towards the center over the filling and start rolling the filling into a cylinder. Repeat with remaining tortillas.
4. Heat ½ inch oil in a large skillet until very hot. Sauté two chimichangas at a time in hot oil until golden, turning with two broad spatulas. Drain on paper toweling; keep warm while cooking remainder. Serve with Green Chile Salsa. Garnish with shredded lettuce and avocado slices, if you wish.

GREEN CHILE SALSA

Makes about 1⅓ cups.

1 can (16-ounces) whole tomatoes, drained
OR: 3 fresh tomatoes, peeled, seeded and chopped
1 can (4 ounces) diced, mild green chilies (½ cup)
½ cup finely chopped green onions
½ teaspoon salt
½ teaspoon leaf oregano, crumbled

Combine all ingredients in a bowl, breaking up canned tomatoes into small pieces. Chill at least 1 hour before serving to blend flavors. Or prepare ahead and store in jar. Refrigerate; use within 1 week.

CHICKEN FLAUTAS

Flauta means flute in Spanish—the perfect name for this tube-shaped taco variation stuffed with mild chile-flavored chicken and eaten out of hand.

Makes 12 flautas.

1 broiler-fryer (about 2½ pounds), cut up
4 cups water
2 tablespoons lard or vegetable shortening
1 medium-size onion, chopped (½ cup)
1 clove garlic, minced
1 tablespoon cornstarch
1¼ teaspoons salt
¼ teaspoon pepper
½ cup canned diced, mild green chilies or to taste (about 4-ounce can)
Vegetable oil for frying
1 dozen fresh or thawed, frozen corn tortillas
1 cup dairy sour cream
¼ cup milk

1. Bring chicken and water to boiling in kettle; lower heat; cover. Simmer until fork tender, about 25 minutes. Drain; reserve ½ cup broth. (Use rest in other recipes.) Cool chicken until easy to handle. Bone and skin chicken; shred meat.
2. Heat lard in a large saucepan until melted. Add onion and garlic; sauté 1 minute. Stir in cornstarch, salt and pepper. Add reserved ½ cup broth, shredded chicken and chilies. Stir and cook until very thick and bubbly; remove from heat.
3. Heat ⅛- to ¼-inch oil in a small skillet over medium heat until very hot. Sauté tortillas one at a time, a few seconds on each side, until limp. This will soften tortillas so that they will roll up more easily. Do not cook too long or they will become crisp. Drain on paper toweling.
4. Fill each tortilla with a heaping spoonful (3 tablespoons) chicken mixture across center. Roll tortilla around filling. Be sure filling is 1 inch from edges or ends of rolled tortilla to avoid splattering during frying.
5. Place 2 or 3 flautas, seam side down, in hot oil. Sauté, turning on all sides, until crisp. Drain. Keep warm while cooking the rest.
6. Combine sour cream and milk in small saucepan. Heat over very low heat just until lukewarm. Spoon over flautas. Garnish with fresh coriander or cilantro leaves, if you wish.

Shortcut Tip: Chicken can be cooked ahead and refrigerated (*see Step 1*). Or use 2¼ cups diced or shredded leftover chicken or pork.

Hawaii

An abundance of fresh fruit and flowers characterizes our Pacific state. The Polynesians, Chinese, Japanese, Filipinos and Portuguese have contributed to this regional cuisine. Savor the flavors of this region with a classic Hawaiian outdoor feast called a luau.

BANANAS HAWAIIAN

Makes 8 servings.

¾ cup flaked coconut
3 tablespoons butter or margarine
½ cup firmly packed brown sugar
1 cup dark rum
¼ teaspoon ground cinnamon
6 bananas, peeled and sliced
1 quart vanilla ice cream

1. Heat coconut in large skillet on grill until toasted; stir to brown evenly. Remove to a sheet of foil; cool.
2. Add butter, sugar, rum and cinnamon to skillet. Heat until bubbly. Add bananas and cook until slices are heated through.
3. Spoon ice cream into serving dishes and spoon hot bananas and juices over. Sprinkle with coconut. Serve at once.

PLUM-GLAZED SPARERIBS

Grill for 30 minutes.
Makes 8 servings.

6 pounds spareribs, cut into 2-rib sections
Water
2 teaspoons salt
1½ pounds fresh red plums
1 cup sugar
⅓ cup cider vinegar
⅓ cup prepared horseradish
1 small onion, finely chopped
1 clove garlic, crushed
1 tablespoon salt

1. Put ribs in large Dutch oven. Add water to cover ribs plus the 2 teaspoons salt. Bring to boiling; lower heat; cover. Simmer 30 minutes or until ribs are almost tender.
2. While ribs are cooking, prepare glaze. Halve, pit and slice plums. Combine with sugar, vinegar, horseradish, onion, garlic and the 1 tablespoon salt in medium-size saucepan. Bring to boiling, stirring often; lower heat. Simmer 5 minutes or until plums are tender.
3. Pour half the plum mixture into container of electric blender; puree until smooth; pour puree into bowl. Repeat with other half. Reserve 1 cup plum mixture in small bowl; chill to serve as dipping sauce.
4. Drain ribs and pat dry with paper toweling. Place in shallow glass or enamel dish. Pour remaining plum mixture over ribs. Let ribs marinate 2 hours at room temperature or in refrigerator overnight.
5. Drain ribs, reserving plum mixture. Place ribs on grill. Grill ribs 30 minutes, turning often and brushing generously with mixture until ribs are browned and evenly glazed. Arrange ribs on platter lined with lemon leaves and garnish with plum halves and canned lychees stuffed with maraschino cherries, if you wish. Serve ribs with reserved plum mixture as a dipping sauce.

Note: If fresh plums are not available, use recipe for Polynesian Glaze instead of the glaze above.

POLYNESIAN GLAZE

Makes about 3 cups.

1 jar (12 ounces) apricot preserves
1 can (8 ounces) crushed pineapple
½ cup catsup
¼ cup cider or wine vinegar
2 tablespoons Worcestershire sauce
1 teaspoon ground ginger
1 teaspoon dry mustard

Combine all ingredients in small saucepan; heat to boiling, stirring constantly. Lower heat; simmer 1 minute. Use to glaze pork or ham.

BUTTERED SWEET POTATOES

Tender golden slices of sweet potato make an excellent accompaniment for either ribs or chicken.

Grill about 35 minutes.
Makes 8 servings.

3 pounds fresh sweet potatoes
⅓ cup butter or margarine
2 teaspoons salt
¼ teaspoon pepper
1 tablespoon chopped parsley

1. Pare sweet potatoes; cut into ¼-inch slices. Place slices on center of a 24-inch length of 18-inch heavy-duty foil or 8 small sheets of foil.
2. Cut butter into small chunks. Place over slices; sprinkle with salt and pepper. Bring ends of foil together evenly; fold over and continue to fold down to top of slices. Fold sides up to make a neat sealed package.
3. Place package directly on hot coals to the side of grill. Grill until potatoes are tender, about 35 minutes, turning package occasionally. Sprinkle slices with parsley before serving.

PINEAPPLE, LUAU STYLE

Grill about 15 minutes.
Makes 8 servings.

1 large ripe pineapple
⅓ cup butter or margarine
⅓ cup honey
2 tablespoons lime juice
¼ teaspoon ground ginger

1. Remove leafy top of pineapple; reserve. Cut pineapple lengthwise into 8 wedges. Cut off core of each wedge. Slash pineapple vertically 1 inch apart down to but not through skin.
2. Heat butter in small saucepan on grill until melted. Add honey, lime juice and ginger. Brush cut surfaces of pineapple with lime mixture. Place wedges on grill. Grill 15 minutes, turning every 5 minutes and brushing with lime mixture.
3. Line serving platter with lemon leaves; place reserved pineapple top in center. Arrange wedges on leaves. Serve hot with remaining lime mixture. Garnish with lime slices, if you wish.

ANCHOVY A small, dark blue or silvery fish found primarily in the Mediterranean Sea but also in some American waters. We are familiar with the ones sold as canned fillets packed in oil or rolled around a caper. (Europeans enjoy fresh anchovies, which can grow to 8 inches long.) The average size is about 3 inches. Some small fish in the herring family are also called anchovies. American anchovies are used as bait rather than fresh food. Because anchovies are so highly perishable, they are salted to preserve them. The curing changes the fresh white flesh to a brownish red. Anchovies are used for flavoring or garnishing foods. Use them in sauces for meat, poultry, eggs and vegetables. They're a popular garnish for veal cutlets, pizza and sandwiches or salads. Store anchovies from an opened can in a jar in the refrigerator. Anchovies are also ground into paste and sold in tubes.

ANGELICA A tall aromatic plant grown in Lapland, Germany, Britain, Spain and France as well as America. Its pale green, celery-like stalks are candied and used to decorate cakes, cookies and candies. The seeds and oil made from the stems and roots are used to flavor liqueurs such as vermouth, chartreuse and Benedictine. Called the "herb of the angels" in ancient times, angelica was believed to ward off the plague.

ANISE An herb plant with the taste of licorice. Native to southwest Asia, Egypt and southeast Europe, it is grown extensively now in Mexico, Spain, Italy and Turkey. The plant has graceful leaves which are used for garnishing and flavoring fruits and vegetables. Fresh anise is limited to those who have home gardens. The seed is dried and used in pastries, candies and flavoring liqueurs.

ANTIPASTO An Italian word, meaning "before the meal." Antipasto foods are usually tart or biting and are served as appetizers before the main course. The most typical antipasto consists of salami, olives, marinated mushrooms, peppers, tuna or anchovies and artichokes. The Italian cured ham, prosciutto, combined with fresh melon or figs is also very popular as an antipasto.

APERITIF A mild alcoholic drink sipped before meals to sharpen the appetite. It is usually a wine or wine-based drink served chilled, on the rocks, straight or with soda water. The word aperitif comes from the Latin meaning "to open". With an aperitif like dry vermouth or dry sherry, you'll open the taste buds for the meal that follows.

APPETIZER Everyone likes a party, especially when there are plenty of appetizers and conviviality. But appetizers are not just for parties. They can be served as the first course of a meal as well. Appetizers are any foods that stimulate the appetite.

Appetizers for a Party

- *Dips* are for dipping, not dripping. Make them thick enough to cling to vegetables, crackers, chips or fruit. Instead of the usual bowl, hollow out vegetables such as eggplant, squash, cabbage, peppers or even a sweet Spanish onion. A fresh hollowed out pineapple makes a nice bowl for a fruit dip.
- *Spreads* should glide over bread or crackers, not shatter them. You can choose from meat or poultry spreads, cheese, seafood or even vegetable spreads.
- *Canapés* are miniature, open-face, hot or cold sandwiches on a base of either bread, pastry, cracker or sliced vegetable. They should be small enough to eat in two bites.
- *Hors d'oeuvres* are any other bite-size finger foods not served on a base.
- *Relishes* such as pickled mushrooms, onions, peppers, olives. Fresh carrot sticks, radishes, green onions and celery are simple relishes.
- *Cheese* with bread, crackers or fruit and nuts can make an easy-on-the-host appetizer. Choose several different-looking cheeses with sharp or very distinct flavors. Let them warm to cool room temperature before serving.

• *Nibblers* are chips, pretzels, nuts or homemade tidbits.

When choosing an appetizer for a first course, consider it as part of the meal. A light appetizer such as a clear soup goes with a heavy meal. An elegant holiday meal requires a special first course, not a jiffy dip and chips. Consider the weather too. Cold finger foods and icy soups are more enjoyable when it's warm outside.

Appetizers for a First Course

- *Fruit or Seafood Cocktail*
- *Pâtés* can be made of meat, poultry, game, seafood or vegetables
- *Soup* can be hot or cold
- *Marinated vegetables or seafood*
- *Smoked fish* such as salmon, trout
- *Pasta* in a light sauce
- *Shellfish* on the half shell

TOASTED TARTARE

All the piquant accompaniments to steak tartare season this broiled beef topping.

Makes 24 canapés.

24 slices party-size rye bread
Butter
1 pound ground round
1 small onion, minced (1/4 cup)
2 egg yolks
2 tablespoons dairy sour cream or heavy cream
2 tablespoons drained capers, mashed
1/2 teaspoon salt
1/4 teaspoon pepper
Chopped fresh parsley

1. Lightly toast bread, on one side only, under broiler. Spread untoasted sides with butter.
2. Combine remaining ingredients, except parsley, in a medium-size bowl and blend well.
3. Mound a generous tablespoonful of the meat mixture on the buttered side of each bread slice. Make sure meat mixture completely covers the bread to prevent burning. Arrange bread on broiler pan.
4. Broil 3 inches from heat for 3 to 4 minutes. Sprinkle with parsley.

Note: Bread can be toasted and buttered and meat mixture can be made ahead of time and refrigerated. Assemble and broil just before serving.

HOMESTYLE BOURSIN

This herbed, garlicky cream cheese has a wonderful flavor and costs less than half the price of the store-bought variety.

Makes 8 servings.

2 packages (8 ounces each) cream cheese, softened
1/4 cup mayonnaise
2 teaspoons Dijon mustard
2 tablespoons finely chopped fresh chives
2 tablespoons finely chopped fresh dill
1 clove garlic, minced

1. Beat cheese, mayonnaise, mustard, chives, dill and garlic with electric mixer in a large bowl until thoroughly blended.
2. Spoon into a small serving bowl or line a 2-cup mold with aluminum foil and spoon in mixture. Cover; refrigerate overnight. Turn out on a small serving plate; peel off foil. Serve with crackers for spreading.

Make-Ahead Tip: Homestyle Boursin may be prepared, covered and refrigerated for up to 4 days before serving.

PEPPERY PICKLED BEANS

Nibblers will be happy with this tasty treat while waiting for the main event.

Makes 2 cups.

1/2 cup water
1/2 cup cider or distilled white vinegar
1 tablespoon salt
1 clove garlic, sliced
1 teaspoon dill seed
1/4 teaspoon cayenne
1 package (9 ounces) frozen cut green beans, thawed

1. Combine water, vinegar, salt, garlic, dill seed and cayenne in a medium-size saucepan. Bring to boiling; add green beans. Bring to boiling again; lower heat; cover and simmer for 5 minutes or until nearly tender (do not overcook). Remove from heat; cool.
2. Pack beans into a pint jar; pour cooking liquid over. Cap tightly and refrigerate for at least 3 days for flavors to develop. Drain well before serving.

CHICKEN PILLOWS

These crisp and garlicky chicken pastries can be put together way ahead of time and frozen, unbaked. Remove from the freezer just before baking.

Bake at 400° for 15 minutes.
Makes about 24 pastries.

2 whole chicken breasts, skinned, boned and halved (about 1 pound)
3 tablespoons lemon juice
2 tablespoons olive or vegetable oil
1 clove garlic, minced
1 teaspoon leaf oregano, crumbled
1/2 teaspoon salt
1/2 cup (1 stick) butter
1/2 package (16-ounce size) phyllo or strudel pastry leaves

1. Cut the chicken into 1-inch cubes.
2. Combine lemon juice, oil, garlic, oregano and salt in a small bowl; mix well. Add the chicken pieces and coat with marinade. Cover and refrigerate overnight.
3. Melt butter over low heat. Unwrap phyllo and place on a piece of wax paper. Keep phyllo covered with another piece of wax paper at all times to prevent drying out. Halve pastry lengthwise with scissors, forming 2 long strips, about 6 inches wide. Take one strip of phyllo, fold in half crosswise and brush with butter. Place 2 pieces of chicken at one short end and roll up in pastry to the midpoint. Fold left and right edges toward the center over filling and continue rolling, forming a neat package. Brush all over with butter and place seam-side down on a jelly-roll pan. Repeat with remaining chicken and phyllo. Preheat oven to 400°.
4. Bake in a preheated hot oven (400°) for 15 minutes or until golden brown.

To Freeze Ahead: Place filled and buttered phyllo rolls on a large baking sheet and freeze. When frozen, transfer to large plastic bags and seal. To bake: Place rolls in a single layer in 2 jelly-roll pans; brush with additional melted butter. Bake in a preheated hot oven (400°) for 20 minutes or until golden brown.

Pictured opposite: American Regional Foods: Hawaiian Barbecue with Plum-Glazed Spareribs, page 12, Buttered Sweet Potatoes, page 13, Pineapple, Luau Style, page 13, and Bananas Hawaiian, page 12

CHICKEN WALNUT STRIPS

Bake at 425° for 15 minutes.
Makes 6 to 8 appetizer servings.

2 whole chicken breasts, skinned, boned and halved (about 1 pound)
2 eggs
Peanut or vegetable oil
½ teaspoon salt
¼ teaspoon pepper
1 cup packaged bread crumbs
1 cup very finely chopped walnuts
Mustard Mayonnaise Dip *(recipe follows)*

1. Cut the chicken breasts into ½ × 3-inch strips with a very sharp knife.
2. Beat the eggs with 1 tablespoon of the oil, salt and pepper in a shallow bowl. Mix the crumbs and nuts on a plate. Preheat oven to 425°.
3. Dip the strips, 1 at a time, in the egg mixture and then coat with the crumbs. Arrange half the strips in a single layer in a jelly-roll pan and pour ¼ cup oil around, not over, them. Repeat with the remaining chicken, arranging in a second pan.
4. Place one pan in center and one in upper third of preheated hot oven (425°); bake for 15 minutes, reversing pan positions after 8 minutes.
5. Turn out on serving plate; serve with Mustard Mayonnaise Dip.

Mustard Mayonnaise Dip: Stir 2 tablespoons Dijon mustard into 1 cup mayonnaise or salad dressing. Cover and chill at least 1 hour before serving.

PIQUANT PICKLED OLIVES

Perk up ripe olives with this spicy marinade.

Makes about 3 cups.

2 cans (5¾ ounces each) pitted ripe olives, drained
2 teaspoons mixed pickling spice
1 large clove garlic, crushed
1 teaspoon crushed red pepper
¼ cup vegetable oil
¼ cup red wine vinegar

Combine all ingredients in a large jar with a screw top; shake gently. Refrigerate several days, shaking jar occasionally. Drain olives just before serving.

CARNITAS CON SALSA

"Carnitas" is Spanish for "little meats." "Salsa" is a spicy fresh tomato sauce. Together, they're terrific!

Bake at 200° for 2 hours.
Makes 10 to 12 appetizer servings.

2 pounds boneless pork shoulder
½ teaspoon salt
¼ teaspoon pepper

Salsa:
1 jar or can (8 ounces) mild taco sauce
1 cup finely chopped peeled, fresh tomatoes
¼ cup finely chopped red onion
¼ cup chopped fresh parsley

1. Trim as much of the fat from the meat as possible with a very sharp knife; cut meat into 1-inch cubes. Arrange in a single layer in a jelly-roll pan; sprinkle with the salt and pepper.
2. Bake in a slow oven (200°) for 2 hours or until crisp and brown.
3. Make Salsa: Combine taco sauce, tomatoes, onion and parsley in a small bowl. Cover and refrigerate.
4. To serve: Center bowl of Salsa on a serving platter and surround with pork cubes for dipping.

CHILE CHEESE SQUARES

This custardy cheese mixture can also be baked in a 9-inch pie plate and served in wedges like a Southwestern quiche.

Bake at 375° for 30 minutes.
Makes about 16 two-inch squares.

1 can (4 ounces) diced, mild green chilies, drained
8 ounces Monterey Jack or sharp Cheddar cheese, shredded (2 cups)
1 cup buttermilk baking mix
1 cup light cream or half-and-half
4 eggs
¼ teaspoon salt
¼ cup sliced pimiento-stuffed olives

1. Sprinkle green chilies and shredded cheese in the bottom of a lightly greased 9-inch square baking pan. Preheat oven to 375°.
2. Combine buttermilk baking mix, cream, eggs and salt in a medium-size bowl; beat until thoroughly blended. Pour over chile-cheese mixture; spread evenly.
3. Bake in a preheated moderate oven (375°) for 30 minutes or until puffed, golden and a skewer inserted in center comes out clean. Let stand 10 minutes before cutting into squares to serve. Garnish squares with olive slices.

To Freeze Ahead: Freeze squares in a single layer on a jelly-roll pan or large baking sheet. Transfer to a plastic bag when frozen. To reheat: Arrange squares in a single layer on a large baking sheet and bake in a moderate oven (350°) for 15 minutes. Garnish as above with pimiento-stuffed olives.

CHINESE PORK AND GINGER BALLS

Makes about 36 meatballs.

1 pound ground pork
1 can (8 ounces) water chestnuts, drained and finely chopped
1 tablespoon finely chopped fresh ginger
OR: 1 teaspoon ground ginger
1 tablespoon soy sauce
1 egg
Peanut or vegetable oil

1. Combine pork, water chestnuts, ginger, soy sauce and egg in medium bowl; blend thoroughly. Shape mixture with wet hands into 1-inch balls.
2. Cover the bottom of a large skillet with oil; heat over medium heat.
3. Place as many meatballs in skillet as will fit without crowding. Cook 5 to 8 minutes, turning often, until crisp and brown and no trace of pink remains on the inside. Transfer meatballs to a serving platter with a slotted spoon; serve immediately.

To Freeze Ahead: Brown meatballs in skillet without cooking all the way through. Freeze in a single layer on baking sheets. When frozen solid, place in a plastic bag; seal. To reheat: Place meatballs in a large baking pan; heat, covered, in a moderate oven (350°) for 30 minutes or until hot and cooked through.

BAMBINI

This is a two-bite version of those giant pizzeria cheese and meat turnovers called calzone.

Bake at 350° for 20 minutes.
Makes 20 turnovers.

1 cup ricotta cheese
½ cup shredded mozzarella cheese
¼ cup grated Parmesan cheese
1 package (10 ounces) large flaky refrigerator biscuits
20 very thin slices pepperoni (half of a 3½-ounce package)

1. Combine ricotta, mozzarella and Parmesan cheeses in a small bowl. Preheat oven to 350°.
2. Halve each biscuit horizontally, forming 20 thin biscuits. If kitchen is hot, refrigerate half the dough while filling the remainder. Gently shape one piece of dough into an oval about 2½ × 4 inches. Place a slice of pepperoni slightly off center on dough. Top with about 1 level tablespoon of cheese mixture. Moisten edges; fold dough over to enclose filling, pinching edges carefully to seal. Transfer to a lightly-greased cookie sheet and repeat with the remaining dough, pepperoni and filling.
3. Bake in a preheated moderate oven (350°) for 20 minutes. Serve warm.

GREEK CUCUMBER DIP

In Greece, this dip is made with thick, rich yogurt. Here, a blend of yogurt plus sour cream is the best way to achieve the authentic flavor and texture of this delicious dipping sauce.

Makes 2½ cups.

2 large cucumbers, pared and coarsely grated
1 cup low-fat yogurt
1 cup dairy sour cream
1 small clove garlic, minced
1 teaspoon salt
¼ teaspoon pepper
Paprika (optional)
Pita Crisps *(recipe follows)*

1. Enclose ¼ of the grated cucumbers in the corner of a clean dish towel and wring out to remove as much moisture as possible. Put the drained cucumbers in a bowl and repeat with the remainder.
2. Stir the yogurt, sour cream, garlic, salt and pepper into the cucumbers. Sprinkle lightly with paprika, if you wish. Serve with Pita Crisps.

Pita Crisps: Split small pita breads in half with scissors, forming two thin rounds. Cut rounds in quarters, place on cookie sheet and bake 7 to 10 minutes at 325° until crisp and very lightly browned.

CREAMY HERBED TUNA DIP

This dip tastes infinitely more exotic than its simple ingredients would indicate.

Makes 1⅓ cups.

1 cup mayonnaise
1 can (3½ ounces) chunk or solid white tuna, drained
1 tablespoon minced onion
1 tablespoon drained capers
¼ cup parsley sprigs
½ teaspoon leaf basil
1 teaspoon lemon juice

1. Place all ingredients in container of electric blender; cover and whirl on medium speed until fairly smooth, stopping machine often to push down contents.
2. Pour into a serving bowl and serve at once, or cover and refrigerate until serving time.

Dipper Tips: Celery sticks or curls, cucumber slices, cherry tomatoes, black olives, hard-cooked eggs, chunks of crusty bread.

APPLE An apple a day may not keep the doctor away, but apples do deliver a lot of health benefits. They are a good source of vitamins A, B and C and also contain minerals like iron and potassium. An average-size apple has only about 80 calories. Another plus: Apples are a natural "toothbrush." They clean your breath, scrub your teeth and massage your gums.

Apples have been cultivated for centuries. The first seeds came to America with the Pilgrims. This versatile fruit can be made into jelly, butter, sauce, juice, sweet or hard cider and even vinegar. Although most apples are harvested in the fall, they are available year round because of commercial storage methods.

Buying and Storing: Look for bright, vibrantly colored apples. No matter what the variety—red, green or yellow—the following tips apply. Avoid apples with a bright, intense green undercast; they are not ripe enough. Don't buy apples with a dull, yellowish-green tinge. They are overripe. The just-ripe apple has a soft, light green cast. Feel apples for firmness and smoothness. Avoid those with bruises, blemishes and breaks. Pick the variety suitable for your purpose. See our chart for the best ways to use different varieties. Sort apples; use the ones with defects first. Apples ripen faster at room temperature. Store apples in plastic bags, in the crisper compartment of the refrigerator, at 32°-40°F. Do not freeze.

Apple Varieties: There are dozens of varieties. Some are best for eating, others are better for cooking or baking. Generally, tart apples are best for cooking, while low-acid varieties like the Red Delicious are preferred for eating or salads. Apple varieties that mature late in the season have somewhat more fiber and tend to hold their shape after cooking better than shorter-growing-season varieties. The best cooking and baking apples are Rome Beauty, York Imperial, R.I. Greening, Granny Smith, Golden Delicious and Northern Spy.

Apple Tidbits: Apples vary in flavor, texture and tartness or sweetness. You may combine several varieties in some apple dishes to get a unique flavor and texture.

Apples retain their shape best if they are simmered—not boiled—in a syrup. Overripe apples tend to mush when cooked. Using apple juice or cider as the cooking liquid helps intensify flavor.

Golden Delicious and Cortland apples stay whiter longer than other varieties. They are good to use in salads and fruit cups. When using other varieties of apples raw, dip the slices in lemon juice or ascorbic-acid mixture to prevent darkening.

Apple Products: *Applesauce* may be

Overleaf: (From left) Carnitas con Salsa, page 16, Bambini, page 17, Chile Cheese Squares, page 16, Chicken Walnut Strips, page 16, Chinese Pork and Ginger Balls, page 16, Toasted Tartare, page 15, and Chicken Pillows, page 15

made from a single variety of apple but is usually a blend of several. *Sliced apples* are pared, cored, sliced and cooked without sugar. They can be used in meat and vegetable dishes as well as desserts. *Apple pie filling* is made of pared, cored, sliced, sweetened and flavored apples, thickened with a starch. Use them for pies and other desserts. *Spiced apple rings* are cored, pared, cooked apples that are sweetened and colored red. *Crab apples* are whole, packed in syrup, spiced and colored. *Apple butter* is concentrated apples with spices. *Apple jelly* is made of juice, pectin, sugar, corn syrup and citric acid. Packaged *dried apples* are great for snacks or for baking or cooking. *Apple juice* and *apple cider* may look alike, but they are two distinct products. Apple juice is filtered many times and pasteurized, resulting in a clear, bland liquid. Cider is filtered fewer times, and may have a cloudy, brownish appearance from the remaining apple pulp. Cider may be pasteurized or benzoate of soda may be added to delay fermentation. Fresh cider, available only during the fall, should be kept under refrigeration and used within a week. Pasteurized juice and cider should be refrigerated after opening. Old-fashioned *hard cider,* an early American favorite, is fermented cider with an alcohol level of about 7%. Hard cider can be distilled into brandy, called *applejack* in this country or *calvados* in Normandy, France.

Apple Math

1 pound apples = 4 small, 3 medium or 2 large
1 pound apples = 3 cups diced or 2¾ cups sliced
2 medium-size apples = 1 cup grated

APPLE VARIETIES AND THEIR USES

Variety	Availability	Range of uses	Notes
McIntosh 3*	Sept.-June	Snacks, salads, fruit cups, sauce and all culinary uses except baked whole. Mildly acid, juicy.	Limited distribution in Far West, South
Red Delicious 3*	Sept.-June	Snacks, salads and fruit cups Sweet, juicy, crisp.	Most universally grown of all apple varieties
Golden Delicious 1*	Sept.-June	Snacks, salads, fruit cups, baking, sauce and all culinary uses. Sweet, juicy, crisp.	Most universally available variety
Rome Beauty 1*	Oct.-June	Snacks, salads, fruit cups, baking and all culinary uses. Very mild flavor.	A fair, fresh eating apple, best for baked and cooked uses
Cortland 3*	Sept.-April	Snacks, salads, fruit cups, baking, sauce and all culinary uses. Firm, slightly acid.	N.E. U.S., Canada and Midwest
Northern Spy 1*	Nov.-May	Snacks, salads, fruit cups, baking and all culinary uses. Moderately tart.	One of finest all-purpose varieties grown. Used extensively in commercial processing.
Granny Smith 1*	All year	Snacks and all culinary purposes. Tart and crisp.	Some grown in West—remainder are imported
Jonathan 3*	Sept.-April	Snacks, salads, fruit cups, sauce and all culinary uses. Mildly tart.	Well distributed except in N.E.
Winesap 2*	Nov.-July	Snacks, salads, baking whole and all culinary uses. Mildly tart, firm, winey taste.	Late-season apple. Excellent keeper.

*Varieties of apples that hold their shape when cooked or baked
1—excellent, 2—good, 3—fair, 4—poor

BAKED APPLE RELISH

A pungent accompaniment to roast chicken.

Bake at 350° for 25 minutes.
Makes 6 servings.

6 small baking apples
2 tablespoons butter or margarine
1 large onion, finely chopped
1 tomato, peeled and chopped (1 cup)
¼ cup raisins
1 tablespoon finely chopped preserved ginger
¼ teaspoon crushed red pepper
¼ teaspoon dry mustard
4 tablespoons red currant jelly
4 tablespoons cider vinegar

1. Cut a slice from top of each apple; remove core with apple corer or small knife. Scoop out apples with the tip of a small spoon, leaving a shell about ½ to ¾-inch thick. Chop the scooped-out apple (about 1 cup).
2. Heat butter in large skillet; add onion and sauté 5 minutes. Stir in chopped apple, tomato, raisins, ginger, crushed red pepper, mustard, 1 tablespoon of the currant jelly and 1 tablespoon of the vinegar. Cook, stirring often, 5 minutes longer or until slightly thickened.
3. Spoon cooked mixture into hollowed-out apples; arrange apples in shallow baking pan. Add remaining jelly and vinegar to skillet; heat just until melted; spoon over and around apples.
4. Bake uncovered and baste once or twice in a moderate oven (350°) for 25 minutes or until apples are glazed and tender. Let cool 15 minutes before serving while basting with juices in pan.

Pictured opposite: Baked Apple Relish, page 20, with roast chicken

CROWN ROAST OF PORK WITH APPLE-HERB STUFFING

A festive roast with a tangy-sweet apple stuffing. You can order a crown roast in advance from the supermarket meat department when pork is the special for the week, or you can follow our directions for preparing a crown roast at home.

Roast at 325° for 3 to 3½ hours.
Makes 8 to 10 servings.

- **1 sixteen-chop crown roast of pork* (about 7 pounds)**
- **1 teaspoon salt**
- **¼ teaspoon pepper**
- **¼ teaspoon leaf sage, crumbled**
- **Apple-Herb Stuffing *(recipe follows)***
- **2 tablespoons light molasses (optional)**
- **2 tablespoons apple or orange juice (optional)**
- **3 tablespoons flour**

1. Place roast, rib ends up, in shallow roasting pan; rub well with mixture of salt, pepper and sage. Insert meat thermometer into meaty portion without touching bone or fat.
2. Roast in a slow oven (325°) for 1½ hours. (Total roasting time based on weight of roast × 35 minutes per pound.) Meanwhile, prepare Apple-Herb Stuffing.
3. Remove roast from oven. Pack stuffing lightly into hollow in the roast, mounding it slightly. Cover stuffing loosely with foil.
4. Return roast to oven; roast 1½ hours longer or until thermometer registers 170°. If you wish, brush roast with mixture of molasses and apple or orange juice several times during last 15 minutes to glaze.
5. Lift roast carefully onto carving board or heated platter with 2 wide spatulas. Keep warm while making gravy.
6. Pour drippings into a 2-cup measure. Let fat rise to top, then skim off. Measure 2 tablespoons of the fat into a small saucepan. Blend in flour; heat until bubbly. Add water to drippings remaining in cup to make 1¾ cups; gradually stir into flour mixture. Cook, stirring constantly until gravy thickens and bubbles 2 minutes. Taste and season with salt and pepper. Serve with Crown Roast. To serve: Slip paper frills over ends of chop bones. Garnish platter with watercress. Carve into chops between ribs, serving a portion of stuffing with each serving.

**To make crown roast yourself, buy 2 rib roasts of pork, 8 ribs on each; have butcher crack backbone so it will be flexible. Trim meat from rib ends ¾- to 1-inch down; place roasts end to end and tie last bone from each together with string at top and bottom. Curve roast to make a ring shape and tie opposite ends together. Tie a string all the way around roast.*

APPLE-HERB STUFFING

This versatile stuffing is excellent with roast chicken, baked ham or braised sausage.

Makes about 5 cups.

- **3 medium-size onions, chopped (1½ cups)**
- **½ cup sliced celery**
- **6 tablespoons butter or margarine**
- **3 cups finely diced baking apples**
- **3 cups whole-wheat bread cubes**
- **¼ cup chopped fresh parsley**
- **½ teaspoon leaf sage, crumbled**
- **½ teaspoon leaf thyme, crumbled**
- **¼ teaspoon ground nutmeg**
- **2 envelopes or teaspoons instant chicken broth**
- **½ cup hot water**

1. Sauté onions and celery in butter in skillet until soft, 5 minutes. Stir in apples; continue cooking and stirring 3 to 5 minutes. Remove from heat.
2. Combine with bread, parsley, sage, thyme, nutmeg, instant chicken broth and water in a large bowl. Toss until evenly moist.

APPLE MOUSSE WITH RASPBERRY-APPLE SAUCE

Makes 8 servings.

- **5 medium-size cooking apples (McIntosh), pared, quartered, cored and sliced (5 cups)**
- **¾ cup sugar**
- **2 envelopes unflavored gelatin**
- **1 cup unsweetened apple juice**
- **1 teaspoon grated lemon rind**
- **2 tablespoons lemon juice**
- **2 egg whites**
- **1 cup heavy cream, whipped**
- **Raspberry-Apple Sauce *(recipe follows)***

1. Combine apples and ½ cup of the sugar in a medium-size saucepan. Bring to boiling; lower heat; cover; simmer 20 minutes or until apples are tender. Purée through food mill or press through sieve over a large bowl. Return to saucepan. Cook over high heat, stirring constantly, until thick, about 5 minutes. Pour the mixture into a large bowl.
2. Soften the gelatin in the apple juice in a small saucepan, 5 minutes. Heat, stirring constantly, over low heat, until gelatin dissolves. Stir into applesauce along with lemon rind and lemon juice. Chill over ice and water, stirring often, until the mixture mounds when spooned.
3. While mixture chills, beat egg whites in small bowl with electric mixer until foamy-white and double in volume. Add remaining ¼ cup sugar, 1 tablespoon at a time, until egg whites stand in soft peaks.
4. Fold meringue and whipped cream into apple mixture until no streaks of white remain. Turn into a 6-cup mold.
5. Refrigerate several hours or until firm; unmold on serving plate. Serve with Raspberry-Apple Sauce.

RASPBERRY-APPLE SAUCE

Makes 1½ cups.

- **1 package (10 ounces) frozen raspberries in quick-thaw pouch, thawed**
- **½ cup unsweetened apple juice**
- **2 tablespoons sugar**
- **2 teaspoons cornstarch**
- **1 tablespoon lemon juice**

1. Combine raspberries and apple juice in container of electric blender; cover. Whirl until smooth. Force mixture through sieve to remove seeds.
2. Combine sugar and cornstarch in medium-size saucepan; stir in raspberry mixture. Cook, stirring constantly, until mixture thickens and clears. Remove from heat; add lemon juice. Pour into small bowl. Refrigerate until cold.

Pictured opposite: Apple Strudel, page 25, Apple Mousse with Raspberry-Apple Sauce, page 22, and Apple Dumplings in Cheese-Walnut Pastry, page 24

CURRIED APPLE AND CHICKEN SOUP

Versatile curry combines well with apple for a smooth colorful soup.

Makes 6 servings.

1 medium-size onion, chopped (½ cup)
¼ cup (½ stick) butter or margarine
2 to 3 cooking apples
2 teaspoons curry powder
1 can condensed cream of chicken soup
2 cups water
½ teaspoon salt
1 cup light cream or half-and-half
1 tablespoon lemon juice

1. Sauté onion in butter in a large saucepan until soft, about 5 minutes. Coarsely shred enough apple to make about 1 cup; add to saucepan; stir in curry powder. Cook and stir 1 to 2 minutes. Add soup; gradually stir in water.
2. Bring to boiling, stirring often; lower heat; cover. Simmer, stirring often, 10 minutes. Puree, ½ at a time, in container of electric blender. Return to saucepan. Add salt and cream and heat through.
3. Shred remaining apple to make about 1 cup; toss with lemon juice; add to soup just before serving.

For Chilled Soup: Add salt and cream to puréed mixture; cool, then chill several hours. Just before serving, shred remaining apple; toss with lemon juice. Garnish with shredded apple.

APPLE PORK LOAF

Bake at 350° for 1¼ hours.
Makes 8 servings.

2 slices whole-wheat bread
½ cup milk
1½ pounds lean ground pork
½ pound pork sausage
1 egg, lightly beaten
½ cup finely diced baking apple
½ cup finely diced celery
¼ cup wheat germ
2 tablespoons chopped fresh parsley
1 teaspoon salt
½ teaspoon pepper
¼ teaspoon leaf basil, crumbled
Pinch leaf thyme
Pinch ground nutmeg
Stir-Fry Apples and Celery *(recipe follows)*

1. Crumble bread into milk in a large bowl. Add pork, sausage, egg, apple, celery, wheat germ, parsley, salt, pepper, basil, thyme and nutmeg; stir until well-blended. Shape into a loaf in shallow baking pan.
2. Bake in a moderate oven (350°) for 1¼ hours. Serve with Stir-Fry Apples and Celery.

STIR-FRY APPLES AND CELERY

2 tablespoons butter or margarine
2 tablespoons vegetable oil
1 tablespoon lemon juice
2 cups thinly sliced celery
2 medium-size cooking apples, quartered, cored and sliced (2 cups)
½ teaspoon salt
¼ teaspoon pepper

1. Heat butter and oil in a large skillet. Add lemon juice and celery; stir-fry over high heat for 5 minutes or until almost tender.
2. Add apples; continue cooking and stirring for 5 minutes or until tender. Sprinkle with salt and pepper.

APPLE DUMPLINGS IN CHEESE-WALNUT PASTRY

Whole apples spiced and sugared and enclosed in a Cheddar cheese pastry.

Bake at 425° for 45 minutes.
Makes 6 servings.

3 cups *sifted* all-purpose flour
1½ teaspoons salt
¾ cup vegetable shortening
2 ounces Cheddar cheese, shredded (½ cup)
¼ cup ground or very finely chopped walnuts
10 to 12 tablespoons ice water
6 medium-size baking apples (Rome Beauty, Granny Smith)
¼ cup (½ stick) butter or margarine, softened
⅓ cup sugar
½ teaspoon apple pie spice OR: A combination of ground cinnamon, nutmeg and cloves
1 egg yolk, slightly beaten
Custard Sauce *(recipe follows)*

1. Sift flour and salt into a medium-size bowl; cut in shortening with a fork or pastry blender until mixture is crumbly; stir in cheese and walnuts.
2. Sprinkle water over mixture; mix lightly with a fork just until pastry holds together and leaves side of bowl clean.
3. Pare apples and core ⅔ way down. Remove any remaining seeds. Combine butter, sugar and apple pie spice in a small bowl until smooth and paste-like. Spoon into centers of apples, dividing evenly.
4. Roll out pastry on a lightly floured surface to a 21×14-inch rectangle; trim excess. Cut into six 7-inch squares; place apple in center of each square. Press pastry firmly around apple. Brush with part of the beaten egg yolk. Place in a 13×9×2-inch baking pan. Preheat oven to 425°.
5. Roll out pastry trimmings; cut out leaf shapes with hors d'ouevre cutter or knife. Cut out six 1×¼-inch wide strips. Press 1 strip on center top of dumpling and arrange leaves around "stem." Brush with remaining beaten egg yolk.
6. Bake in a preheated hot oven (425°) for 45 minutes or until apples are tender and pastry is golden. Serve warm with Custard Sauce.

CUSTARD SAUCE

Makes 2½ cups.

4 egg yolks
¼ cup sugar
2 teaspoons cornstarch
2 cups milk, scalded
1 teaspoon vanilla

Beat egg yolks with sugar and cornstarch in a medium-size bowl; gradually stir in milk. Pour into medium-size saucepan; cook over moderate heat, stirring constantly, until custard thickens slightly and coats a spoon. Remove from heat; pour into a small bowl; stir in vanilla; cover. Chill.

APPLE STRUDEL

Crispy pastry with a buttery apple-nut filling.

Bake at 400° for 35 minutes.
Makes 2 strudels.

1 cup fresh bread crumbs (2 slices bread)
1 cup ground walnuts
8 medium-size cooking apples (McIntosh, Golden Delicious), pared, quartered, cored and thinly sliced (8 cups)
1 cup sugar
1 cup golden raisins
1 teaspoon grated lemon rind
1 tablespoon lemon juice
1 teaspoon ground cinnamon
16 strudel or phyllo leaves (from a 16-ounce package)
¾ cup (1½ sticks) unsalted butter, melted
10X (confectioners') sugar

1. Combine bread crumbs and walnuts in a large skillet and stir over medium-high heat until crumbs and nuts are golden, about 5 minutes. Remove from heat.
2. Combine apples, sugar, raisins, lemon rind, lemon juice and cinnamon in a large bowl.
3. Place 4 strudel leaves on a clean towel; place another 4 leaves overlapping to form an 18×18-inch square of dough.
4. Brush dough completely with some of the melted butter. Sprinkle half of the crumb-nut mixture over entire surface.
5. Spoon half of the apple mixture in an even row down one side of the dough, 2 inches in from edges.
6. Using the towel, lift dough up and over filling. Fold the two adjacent sides of the dough toward center, in order to completely enclose the apple filling.
7. Continue rolling strudel, aided by towel; allow it to roll over and over on itself until completely rolled. (You will have a 15×3-inch roll.) Preheat oven to 400°.
8. Carefully ease filled roll onto a jelly-roll pan; repeat for remaining apple strudel.
9. Bake in a preheated hot oven (400°) for 35 minutes, brushing several times with remaining butter.
10. Allow strudel to cool 15 minutes before removing to serving board. Sprinkle with 10X sugar.

APPLE-ALMOND TART

Bake at 350° for 10 minutes, and then for 35 minutes.
Makes 6 servings.

1¼ cups *sifted* all-purpose flour
¼ cup slivered blanched almonds, toasted and ground
⅛ teaspoon salt
¼ cup sugar
½ cup (1 stick) cold unsalted butter
2 egg yolks, lightly beaten
1 teaspoon vanilla
4 Granny Smith or other tart apples (about 1½ pounds)
½ cup sugar
1 tablespoon lemon juice
2 tablespoons water
¼ cup slivered blanched almonds
2 tablespoons apple jelly

1. Combine flour, ground almonds, salt and the ¼ cup sugar in a medium-size bowl. Cut in butter with a pastry blender until mixture is crumbly. Stir in egg yolks and vanilla until blended. Gather dough into a ball. Flatten dough and press into a 9-inch tart pan with removable bottom. Chill 30 minutes. Prick bottom of shell with fork. Preheat oven to 350°.
2. Bake in a preheated moderate oven (350°) for 10 minutes. Remove from oven to wire rack.
3. Pare, core and cut apples into slices. Cook 2 cups of the slices, ¼ cup of the sugar, lemon juice and water in a medium-size saucepan, stirring occasionally, until apples are soft, about 20 minutes. Beat with a spoon; cool. Spread apple sauce over bottom of pastry shell.
4. Toss remaining apple slices with remaining ¼ cup sugar. Arrange slices on top of the apple sauce. Sprinkle with slivered almonds.
5. Bake in a moderate oven (350°) for 35 minutes, or until apples are tender.
6. Place tart under broiler with top 3 to 4 inches from heat until apples are lightly browned. Remove to wire rack. Melt apple jelly in a small saucepan over low heat; brush over top of slices to glaze. Cool completely.

THE PERFECT APPLE PIE

Bake at 425° for 40 minutes.
Makes one 9-inch pie.

2½ pounds cooking apples, pared, quartered, cored and thinly sliced (8 cups)
⅓ cup firmly-packed light brown sugar
⅓ cup granulated sugar
1 tablespoon cornstarch
OR: 2½ tablespoons flour
1 teaspoon ground cinnamon
¼ teaspoon ground nutmeg
¼ teaspoon salt
1 package piecrust mix
2 tablespoons butter or margarine
Water or milk
Sugar

1. Place apples in a large bowl; mix sugars, cornstarch, cinnamon, nutmeg and salt in a small bowl; sprinkle over apples; toss gently to mix. Let stand until a little juice forms, about 10 minutes.
2. Meanwhile, prepare piecrust mix, following label directions. Roll out ½ of dough to 12-inch round on lightly floured surface; fit into 9-inch pie plate. Trim overhang to ½ inch.
3. Roll out remaining pastry for top to 12-inch round; fold into quarters; make 3 slits near center in each of folded edges for steam to escape. Pile apple mixture into pastry; dot with butter. Moisten edge of bottom pastry with water. Place folded pastry on apples so point is on center; unfold. Trim overhang to 1 inch; turn edges under and press together to seal. Pinch to make stand-up edge; flute or make your favorite edging. Preheat oven to 425°.
4. For a crispy-sugary top, brush top of pastry with a little water or milk and sprinkle lightly with sugar.
5. Bake pie in a preheated hot oven (425°) for 40 minutes, or until juices bubble through slits and apples are tender. If edge is browning too fast, cover with a narrow strip of foil. Serve warm with scoops of vanilla ice cream or chunks of Cheddar cheese.

APPLE-CARROT TOSS

Makes 8 servings.

- **4 medium-size eating apples, quartered, cored and diced (4 cups)**
- **2 large carrots, shredded**
- **½ cup coarsely chopped walnuts**
- **1 container (8 ounces) dairy sour cream**
- **2 tablespoons lemon juice**
- **3 tablespoons 10X (confectioners') sugar**
- **½ teaspoon salt**
- **½ teaspoon ground ginger**
- **½ small head iceberg lettuce, shredded**

1. Combine apples, carrots and walnuts in a medium-size bowl.
2. Blend sour cream, lemon juice, 10X sugar, salt and ginger in a small bowl; pour over apple-carrot mixture; toss lightly to mix. Let stand about 15 minutes to season.
3. Place lettuce in a shallow serving bowl; spoon apple mixture on top; toss lightly to mix.

•●•

APRICOT One of the first fresh fruits of summer, apricots are also canned and dried for year-round eating. Apricots traveled the globe westward from China through Persia and the Mediterranean area, to England, where the Arab spelling "alburquq" was changed to "abricock" and later to the present word. The Spaniards brought the fruit to Mexico, and northward to the missions in California in the early 18th century. California now produces most of the apricots on the market.

Buying and Storing: Fresh apricots appear late in May or early in June and last through early August. Canned apricots are sold whole, peeled or unpeeled; halved, peeled or unpeeled. They are packed in syrup, water or juice.

It takes six pounds of fresh apricots to yield one pound of dried apricots. Dried apricots are costly, but their ambrosial flavor makes up for the expense. A little goes a long way toward flavoring coffee cakes, desserts and even main dishes.

Keep fresh apricots at room temperature until fully ripe, then refrigerate. To ripen apricots quickly, place in a closed paper bag in a warm room. Canned apricots should be refrigerated once they are opened. Dried apricots, sold in packages or boxes, should be placed in an airtight container and refrigerated after opening.

Apricot Nutrition: An excellent source of vitamins A and C. A half cup of fresh apricot halves has only 36 calories. The same amount canned in syrup has 110 calories.

Apricot Math

- 1 pound fresh apricots=12 medium or 3 cups sliced
- 1 can (17 ounces) halves=10 to 12 halves or 1 cup fruit
- 1 package (8 ounces) dried large halves=42 to 45 halves or 1⅔ cups

APRICOT-WHEAT GERM-CORN BREAD

Bake at 375° for 40 minutes.
Makes 2 small loaves.

- **⅔ cup *sifted* all-purpose flour**
- **⅓ cup sugar**
- **3½ teaspoons baking powder**
- **1 teaspoon salt**
- **⅔ cup wheat germ**
- **⅔ cup yellow cornmeal**
- **¾ cup chopped dried apricots**
- **2 eggs**
- **1 cup milk**
- **¼ cup vegetable oil**

1. Sift flour, sugar, baking powder and salt into a medium-size bowl. Stir in wheat germ, cornmeal and apricots. Preheat oven to 375°.
2. Beat eggs slightly in a small bowl. Stir in milk and oil.
3. Pour liquid ingredients into dry and stir just until flour is evenly moist. Spoon batter into 2 greased 7⅜ × 3⅝ × 2¼-inch loaf pans.
4. Bake in a preheated moderate oven (375°) for 40 minutes or until wooden pick inserted in the centers comes out clean. Cool in pans on wire rack 10 minutes. Remove from pans; cool completely. Wrap in foil or plastic when cool; store overnight for easier slicing.

APRICOT CHARLOTTE BOMBE

A spectacular dessert with five ingredients that go together like a breeze.

Makes 6 servings.

- **1 can (16 ounces) whole apricots**
- **⅓ cup apricot preserves**
- **1 pint ice cream (vanilla, chocolate or your favorite flavor)**
- **7 to 8 ladyfingers, split**
- **Thawed, frozen whipped topping or whipped cream**

1. Drain apricots, reserving 1 tablespoon syrup. Heat preserves with syrup in small saucepan until melted.
2. Unmold ice cream from carton in one piece onto a chilled serving plate. Press ladyfingers onto side and top of ice cream to cover completely, cutting to fit where necessary. Brush melted preserve mixture over ladyfingers until absorbed. Return to freezer.
3. Just before serving, arrange apricots on plate and decorate with whipped topping.

APRICOT SAUCE

Makes 1½ cups.

- **1 can (8¾ ounces) apricot halves**
- **1 can (12 ounces) apricot nectar**
- **2 teaspoons cornstarch**
- **½ cup toasted slivered or sliced blanched almonds**
- **1 tablespoon golden or dark rum**

1. Drain apricot halves, reserving syrup. Slice halves.
2. Add enough apricot nectar to reserved apricot syrup to measure 1½ cups. Pour all but 1 tablespoon into a medium-size saucepan; heat over low heat.
3. Blend cornstarch with reserved tablespoon syrup in a cup; stir into saucepan. Bring to boiling; lower heat; simmer 1 minute, stirring constantly, until thickened and clear. Add apricot slices; simmer 1 more minute on low heat. Remove from heat. Add toasted almonds and rum. Serve over ice cream or pound cake slices.

Pictured opposite: Apricot Charlotte Bombe, page 27

APRICOT-COCONUT COOKIE BARS

Bake at 350° for 25 minutes, and then for 35 minutes.
Makes about 40 bars.

½ cup (1 stick) butter, softened
¼ cup sugar
1⅓ cups *sifted* all-purpose flour
½ teaspoon baking powder
¼ teaspoon salt
2 eggs, well beaten
1 can (15 ounces) sweetened condensed milk
1 can (3½ ounces) flaked coconut
1 package (6 ounces) dried apricots, finely chopped

1. Preheat oven to 350°. Place the butter, sugar and 1 cup of the flour in a medium-size bowl. Cut in butter with pastry blender until coarse crumbs form.
2. Press crumbs firmly onto the bottom of a buttered 9-inch square baking pan to make a bottom crust.
3. Bake in a preheated moderate oven (350°) for 25 minutes. Remove from oven to wire rack.
4. Combine remaining ⅓ cup flour, baking powder, salt, eggs, condensed milk, coconut and apricots in a medium-size bowl; mix until well blended. Spread mixture evenly over baked cookie layer.
5. Bake in a preheated moderate oven (350°) for 35 minutes or until top is firm to the touch. Cool in pan on wire rack. Cut into 2 × 1-inch bars.

APRICOT CREAM

Makes 2½ cups.

1 cup dried apricots, chopped coarsely
1 cup water
⅓ cup honey
½ teaspoon salt
1 container (16 ounces) dairy sour cream (2 cups)
Toasted slivered almonds

1. Cook apricots in water in a small saucepan until tender, about 10 minutes. Drain well; cool.
2. Combine honey, salt and sour cream in bowl; stir in cooled apricots. Chill before serving. Garnish with almonds.

APRICOT CAKE ROLL

Bake at 375° for 12 to 15 minutes.
Makes 1 jelly roll.

1 cup *sifted* cake flour
1 teaspoon baking powder
¼ teaspoon salt
3 eggs
¾ cup sugar
⅓ cup water
1 teaspoon vanilla
10X (confectioners') sugar
¾ cup apricot preserves

1. Grease a 15½ × 10½ × 1-inch jelly-roll pan; line bottom with wax paper; grease paper.
2. Sift flour, baking powder and salt. Preheat oven to 375°.
3. Beat eggs in a medium-size bowl with electric mixer until thick and creamy. Gradually add sugar, beating constantly until mixture is very thick. (This will take at least 5 minutes.) Blend in water and vanilla on low speed. Add flour mixture, beating (on low speed) just until batter is smooth. Pour into prepared pan, spreading evenly into corners.
4. Bake in a preheated moderate oven (375°) for 12 minutes or until center of cake springs back when lightly pressed with fingertip.
5. Loosen cake around edges with a small knife; invert onto a clean towel dusted with 10X sugar; peel off wax paper. Starting at short end, roll up cake and towel together. Cool on wire rack. When cool, unroll carefully; spread evenly with preserves. Reroll cake. Place seam side down on platter or small cookie sheet until ready to slice and serve.

•●•

ARROWROOT A plant grown in the West Indies whose root yields a starch used to thicken sauces. Arrowroot is sold in powder form. Use it as an alternative to flour or cornstarch to thicken sauces, puddings, soups and gravies. It is also used in cookies.

ARROZ The Spanish word for rice.

ARROZ CON POLLO

Spain's classic chicken bakes neatly in a casserole together with golden saffron, rice, tomatoes, and peas. With canned and frozen foods trimming preparation time, it's oven-ready in minutes.

Broil for 8 to 10 minutes; bake at 375° for 45 minutes, and then for 15 minutes.
Makes 6 servings.

1 broiler-fryer (about 3 pounds), cut up
3 tablespoons olive oil
1 teaspoon salt
¼ teaspoon pepper
½ teaspoon paprika
1 cup frozen chopped onion
1 clove garlic, crushed
¼ teaspoon crushed saffron
½ teaspoon leaf oregano, crumbled
1 cup water
1 can (16 ounces) tomatoes, undrained
2 envelopes or teaspoons instant chicken broth
1 bay leaf
1¼ cups uncooked long-grain rice
1 package (10 ounces) frozen peas, thawed
1 canned pimiento, slivered

1. Rub chicken pieces with 1 tablespoon of the olive oil, then sprinkle with ¼ teaspoon of the salt, ⅛ teaspoon of the pepper and all of the paprika. Place skin side up on a foil-lined shallow baking pan and broil, 5 inches from the heat, 8 to 10 minutes or until nicely browned.
2. Meanwhile, sauté onion and garlic in a large heavy skillet over fairly high heat in remaining 2 tablespoons olive oil 3 to 4 minutes until limp. Mix in saffron and oregano and heat, stirring, 1 to 2 minutes. Stir in water, tomatoes, instant chicken broth, bay leaf, remaining ¾ teaspoon salt and ⅛ teaspoon pepper. Simmer 1 to 2 minutes, breaking up tomatoes; add rice and bring to boiling, continuing to stir.
3. Pour all into a 3-quart casserole; arrange browned chicken pieces on top, pushing them down into liquid slightly. Cover.
4. Bake in a moderate oven (375°) for 45 minutes or until rice is almost ten-

der and almost all liquid is absorbed. Fork up rice mixture a bit; add peas and pimiento, distributing them attractively in and around chicken pieces and pushing most of them down into rice mixture. Re-cover and bake 15 minutes longer until peas are cooked through. Remove bay leaf.

•●•

ARTICHOKE A green, thistle-like vegetable which consists of the leaves, the inedible choke, and the heart or bottom. See also **JERUSALEM ARTICHOKE.**

Buying and Storing: California supplies most of the artichokes purchased in the United States. Choose firm, compact, blemish-free heads. Allow 1 medium-large size for a serving.

Besides fresh artichokes, frozen, canned and marinated hearts are available.

To Cook: Simmer, covered, in salted water for 35 to 40 minutes or until leaves pull away easily.

To Microwave: Put 1 cup water and dash salt in large casserole dish. Add 4 medium artichokes. Cover. Microwave on high power 7 minutes. Rotate dish; microwave 7 to 8 minutes more or until a leaf can be pulled off easily. Drain artichokes upside down.

How to eat an artichoke: Pull the leaves off one at a time and dip fleshy base into melted butter or sauce. Pull the leaf between your teeth to scrape off the pulp. Discard the rest of the leaf. Continue until you reach the fuzzy choke. Remove the choke with a sharp knife. Cut up the heart and dip into sauce.

ARTICHOKES WITH MUSTARD SAUCE

Makes 6 servings.

6 medium-size artichokes
1 teaspoon salt
1 tablespoon vegetable oil
1 small clove garlic, crushed
3 tablespoons butter or margarine
3 tablespoons flour
1 tablespoon prepared mustard
1 envelope or teaspoon instant chicken broth
1½ cups water
1 tablespoon lemon juice

1. Wash artichokes in cold water; cut 1 inch off top, straight across. Cut off stem 1 inch from base. With scissors cut off thorny tip of each leaf.
2. Place artichokes standing upright in a single layer in a large kettle; fill kettle to a depth of 1 inch with boiling water; add ½ teaspoon of the salt and oil to water. Cover; simmer 35 to 40 minutes, or until leaves pull out easily and base of artichoke can be easily pierced with a fork. Drain upside down on wire rack.
3. Sauté garlic in butter 1 minute; stir in flour; cook, stirring constantly, just until bubbly; stir in mustard, instant chicken broth, and the remaining ½ teaspoon salt until well blended. Stir in water; cook, stirring constantly, until sauce thickens and bubbles 1 minute; stir in lemon juice.
4. To eat artichokes, pull off leaves, one at a time, dip base in sauce, then scrape off its tender flesh with teeth; remove and discard fuzzy choke; cut the artichoke bottom with a knife and dip into sauce.

ARTICHOKE AND CELERY SALAD

Makes 6 servings.

1 package (9 ounces) frozen artichoke hearts, thawed
1 cup chopped celery
2 tablespoons minced green onion
2 canned pimientos, cut into strips
½ teaspoon dry mustard
½ teaspoon salt
¼ teaspoon pepper
2 tablespoons red wine vinegar
6 tablespoons vegetable oil
Lettuce greens or watercress

1. Combine artichokes in a bowl with celery, green onion and pimientos.
2. Mix mustard, salt, pepper, vinegar and oil in small bowl or measuring cup. Pour over artichokes; toss gently; cover bowl. Marinate in refrigerator for several hours.
3. To serve: Divide into six portions on individual salad plates lined with lettuce or watercress.

ARTICHOKE SPECIAL

Bake at 350° for 20 minutes.
Makes 4 servings.

2 packages (9 ounces each) frozen artichoke hearts
2 green onions, chopped
2 tablespoons butter
¼ pound fresh mushrooms, chopped (1 cup)
1 clove garlic, minced
¾ cup fresh bread crumbs
½ teaspoon salt
¼ teaspoon leaf basil, crumbled
Freshly ground pepper
5 ounces mild Cheddar cheese, shredded (1¼ cups)
2 eggs
½ cup dairy sour cream
2 tablespoons butter, melted

1. Thaw artichokes by running water over them until they separate. Arrange in single layer in shallow greased 6-cup baking dish.
2. Sauté onions in 2 tablespoons of the butter in large skillet until soft, about 5 minutes. Add mushrooms and garlic; cook 5 minutes. Remove from heat; set aside.
3. Stir ½ cup of the bread crumbs, salt, basil, pepper and 1 cup of the cheese into mushroom mixture.
4. Beat eggs in small bowl with sour cream. Stir into skillet until well blended. Spread over artichokes in the baking dish.
5. Combine remaining ¼ cup crumbs with remaining ¼ cup cheese. Sprinkle over top of casserole. Drizzle with the remaining melted butter.
6. Bake, uncovered, in a moderate oven (350°) for 20 minutes, or until artichokes are tender when pierced with a fork.

•●•

ASPARAGUS A quick-cooking, succulent vegetable which is low in calories (22 calories in 6 spears) and low in sodium. Enjoy the spears simply boiled or steamed, or cut up and stir-fried. Asparagus is also delicious in soups and salads.

Asparagus is cultivated in northern California and in Oregon for sale in the spring. New Jersey provides early summer spears. Asparagus

which is grown away from sunlight does not turn green and is sold, in cans, as white asparagus.

Tips for Buying: Select firm, green stalks with tightly closed tips. Ends should not be woody. Fresh asparagus does not keep well. Refrigerate and use within a few days. Allow 6 to 8 spears per serving. Asparagus is also available canned and frozen.

To Prepare: Snap off tough ends; wash stalks under cold running water. Snip large or sandy scales with a sharp knife and wash again. Or pare the outer skin from the lower portion of the stalks with a potato peeler.

To Cook Whole: Tie stalks with string in serving-size bundles. Bring lightly salted water to boiling in a large skillet; add asparagus. When water returns to boil, reduce heat, cover and simmer 10 to 13 minutes or until lower part of stalks is tender. Drain bundles well on paper toweling. OR: Stand bundles upright in a deep saucepan. Pour boiling water to a depth of 2 inches. Add dash salt; cover. Cook and drain as above. (A clean coffee percolator is perfect for this. Or, use a double boiler with the insert inverted as a cover.)

To Cook Cut-Up: Cut spears into 1½-inch lengths. Drop into boiling salted water. Cook, covered 3 to 5 minutes or just until tender and still bright green. If serving cold, rinse with cold water to stop cooking. Drain well on paper toweling.

To Microwave Spears: In 12×8-inch dish, combine ¼ cup water and dash salt. Arrange 1 pound of spears in dish so that tips face the center. Cover with vented plastic wrap; microwave on high power 4 minutes. Rotate outside stalks to the middle; keep tips in center. Microwave covered 2½ to 5½ minutes.

To Microwave Cut-Up: Put ¼ cup water and dash salt in 2-quart casserole. Add cut-up asparagus. Cover. Microwave on high power 3 minutes. Stir and microwave covered until tender.

Asparagus Math

1 pound=16 to 20 stalks=2 to 3 servings

PASTA WITH ASPARAGUS

Makes 6 servings.

2 pounds asparagus
1 package (1 pound) very thin spaghetti
6 bacon slices, cut in 1-inch pieces
⅓ cup chopped green onions
½ teaspoon pepper
¼ cup (½ stick) butter or margarine
½ cup light cream or half-and-half
½ cup grated Parmesan cheese

1. Wash and trim asparagus; cut into 1-inch diagonal pieces. Partially cook in boiling salted water to cover, 3 minutes. Drain.
2. Cook spaghetti following package directions; drain and return to kettle.
3. Cook bacon in a large skillet until crisp; stir in onions and pepper. Add asparagus and toss to coat.
4. Add butter and cream to spaghetti; toss to coat evenly; add Parmesan; toss well. Add asparagus mixture and toss gently to distribute evenly. Serve with additional cheese, if you wish.

STIR-FRIED ASPARAGUS

Makes 6 servings.

1½ pounds asparagus
2 tablespoons peanut or vegetable oil
2 teaspoons finely chopped fresh ginger
OR: ½ teaspoon ground ginger
1 clove garlic, finely chopped
⅛ to ¼ teaspoon crushed red pepper
¼ cup broken walnuts
¼ cup slivered sweet red pepper
2 tablespoons soy sauce
2 tablespoons dry sherry
½ teaspoon sugar
½ teaspoon salt

1. Wash and trim asparagus; slice on the diagonal, making long thin slices.
2. Heat oil in large skillet; stir-fry asparagus just until crisp-tender, about 2 minutes. Remove from skillet with slotted spoon.
3. Stir ginger, garlic and crushed red pepper into skillet. Add walnuts and sweet red pepper; cook and stir 1 minute. Add soy sauce, sherry, sugar and salt. Return asparagus to skillet; toss to heat through.

CREAM OF ASPARAGUS SOUP

Velvety smooth with the fresh taste of just-cooked asparagus.

Makes 6 servings.

2 pounds asparagus
1 small onion, finely chopped
¼ cup (½ stick) butter or margarine
2 tablespoons flour
1 can (13¾ ounces) chicken broth
1 cup heavy cream
⅛ teaspoon ground nutmeg

1. Wash and trim asparagus; cut into 1-inch pieces. Cook in boiling salted water to cover just until tender, 10 to 13 mintues. Drain, reserving 1½ cups of the cooking water.
2. Place cooked asparagus and reserved liquid in container of electric blender; whirl until mixture is smooth.
3. Sauté onion in butter in large saucepan until tender but not brown, about 3 minutes. Stir in flour; cook over low heat until bubbly, about 1 minute. Gradually stir in chicken broth. Bring to boiling, stirring constantly. Lower heat; simmer 3 minutes. Add asparagus puree, ½ cup of the cream and the nutmeg. Bring just to boiling.
4. Whip remaining cream in a small bowl until soft peaks form. Serve soup hot or cold with a dollop of cream on each serving.

LEMON-BUTTERED ASPARAGUS

Makes 4 to 6 servings.

2 to 2½ pounds asparagus
2 tablespoons fresh lemon juice
8 tablespoons (1 stick) butter or margarine
Lemon wedges

1. Wash and trim asparagus. Cook in boiling water just until tender, 10 to 13 minutes.
2. Combine lemon juice and 2 tablespoons of butter in a small saucepan; heat until bubbly. Gradually add remaining butter, stirring until blended.
3. Drain asparagus. Arrange on platter. Spoon lemon butter over asparagus.Garnish with lemon wedges.

Pictured opposite: Lemon-Buttered Asparagus, page 31

Asparagus

ASPARAGUS VINAIGRETTE

Makes 6 servings.

2½ pounds asparagus
⅔ cup olive or vegetable oil
⅓ cup white wine vinegar
½ teaspoon Dijon mustard
½ teaspoon salt
⅛ teaspoon pepper
1 tablespoon chopped fresh parsley
1 tablespoon chopped green onion
1 tablespoon sweet pickle relish
1 tablespoon chopped pimiento

1. Wash and trim asparagus. Cook until just tender, 10 to 13 minutes; drain. Rinse with cold water to stop cooking; drain on paper toweling. Arrange on platter; chill.
2. Combine oil, vinegar, mustard, salt, pepper, parsley, onion, relish and pimiento in jar with screw-top. Shake well. Chill 2 hours for flavors to develop.
3. Spoon dressing over asparagus about ½ hour before serving.

•●•

ASPIC A clear, savory gelatin made from vegetable, meat, fish or poultry broth. It is used for coating or glazing cold foods, or to make molds in which vegetables, fish, cooked eggs, meat or poultry are suspended. It's also cut into cubes or decorative shapes and used as garnish.

DILLED SHRIMP IN ASPIC

Makes 6 servings.

1 package (1 pound) frozen shelled, deveined shrimp
1 medium-size cucumber
2 tablespoons chopped fresh dill
1 tablespoon minced onion
2 tablespoons lemon juice
½ teaspoon salt
⅛ teaspoon pepper
2 cans (13¾ ounces each) chicken broth
2 envelopes unflavored gelatin
2 tablespoons lemon juice
Canned pimiento
Fresh dill sprigs
Creamy Dressing *(recipe follows)*

1. Cook shrimp, following package directions; drain; cool. Pick out several even-size shrimp; reserve for decoration. Cut remaining shrimp into ¼-inch pieces; place in a medium-size bowl.
2. Cut half the cucumber into very thin slices; reserve for decoration. Pare and seed remaining half of cucumber; cut into ½-inch pieces; place in bowl with diced shrimp. Stir in chopped dill, onion, 2 tablespoons of the lemon juice, salt, and pepper. Let stand 1 hour to season. Drain well.
3. Skim fat from chicken broth; discard. Soften gelatin in 1 cup of the broth about 5 minutes in a small saucepan. Heat, stirring constantly, until gelatin dissolves; stir into remaining chicken broth in a medium-size bowl. Add remaining 2 tablespoons lemon juice. Cut out decorative shapes from pimiento.
4. Pour ½ cup of the gelatin mixture into bottom of a 6-cup ring mold; place in a large bowl filled with mixture of ice and water until mixture is sticky-firm. Quickly arrange reserved shrimp, cucumber slices, pimiento cutouts and sprigs of dill in aspic in bottom of mold; spoon several tablespoons of liquid aspic over decorations. Chill again until sticky-firm.
5. Chill remaining gelatin mixture until as thick as unbeaten egg white in bowl of ice and water to speed setting. Stir in drained shrimp and cucumber mixture; gently spoon over decorated layer in ring mold; chill until firm, at least 4 hours or overnight.
6. Just before serving, loosen salad around edge with a knife; dip mold very quickly in and out of hot water; wipe off water. Cover pan with serving plate; turn upside-down; shake gently; lift off mold. Border with reserved cucumber slices, halved. Top with Creamy Dressing.

Creamy Dressing: Combine ½ cup dairy sour cream; ½ cup mayonnaise or salad dressing; ½ teaspoon salt; ¼ teaspoon celery seeds, crushed; and ¼ teaspoon dry mustard in a small bowl; stir to blend well. Cover; refrigerate at least 1 hour to blend flavors. Makes about 1 cup.

TOMATO ASPIC

Good with cold sliced meats or salad greens as a first course.

Makes 4 cups.

2 envelopes unflavored gelatin
2½ cups tomato juice
1 can condensed beef broth
¼ cup lemon juice
¼ teaspoon liquid hot pepper seasoning
Watercress and lemon slices
Cucumber Yogurt Dressing *(recipe follows)*

1. Sprinkle gelatin over 1 cup of the tomato juice in medium-size saucepan. Heat slowly, stirring until gelatin dissolves.
2. Remove from heat; stir in remaining 1½ cups tomato juice, beef broth, lemon juice and liquid hot pepper. Pour into 4-cup mold or individual molds.
3. Chill until firm, at least 4 hours. Unmold onto serving plate. Garnish with watercress and lemon. Serve with Cucumber Yogurt Dressing.

Cucumber Yogurt Dressing: Strain 1 container (8 ounces) plain yogurt to remove extra liquid. Combine strained yogurt with 2 tablespoons chopped, pared, seeded cucumber and 6 chopped stuffed green olives; chill. Makes about 1 cup.

•●•

AVOCADO The avocado, or alligator pear, is a fruit with buttery-textured, nutty-tasting flesh. It may be chopped or sliced into a salad, or blended into a delicious, creamy soup—even a dessert mousse.

Avocados are grown in the tropical climes of California and Florida. Size varies greatly, the smallest being egg-sized, the largest weighing up to 3 pounds. Appearance varies as well. The California Fuerte variety, available from October to May, is green, thin-skinned, weighing 8 to 16 ounces. The Hass variety, sold from May to October, has a dark, pebbly skin. Florida varieties are generally larger than California avocados. They are light green and smooth-skinned, sold July to January.

Tips for Buying: Hold an avocado in your hands and gently press the

Pictured opposite: Tomato Aspic, page 32

ends. If it yields to gentle pressure, it's ripe and ready. It's best to plan ahead and buy several unripe avocados. Let them stand at room temperature until they ripen. Then refrigerate and use within a few days. You can freeze the pulp if it has been mashed with a little lemon juice to prevent discoloration.

Avocado Nutrition: Avocados have a high fat content, most of which is unsaturated. One-half an 8-ounce avocado has 150 calories and provides vitamin C, riboflavin, magnesium and potassium.

To Prepare: Cut avocado lengthwise around the pit in the center. Rotate the halves in opposite directions to separate. Remove pit. Brush cut surfaces with lemon juice, dilute vinegar or ascorbic-acid mixture to reduce discoloration. Serve on the half shell, or peel and slice or cube.

Avocado Math

1 small=⅓ to ½ cup puree or 12 bite-size cubes

1 avocado (16 ounces)=about 1 cup puree

AVOCADO WHIP

Especially refreshing. Serve as a party dessert with thin butter cookies.

Makes 4 servings.

1 large avocado
2 tablespoons lemon juice
2 tablespoons sugar
½ pint (1 cup) vanilla ice cream, softened

1. Halve avocado; pit and peel. Cut into small pieces, then mash in a medium-size bowl with a fork until smooth, sprinkling with the lemon juice to prevent darkening. Stir in sugar. (You should have 1 cup of avocado mixture.)
2. Spoon softened ice cream into avocado mixture. Beat with electric mixer until well mixed, but do not let ice cream melt.
3. Spoon into stemmed glasses and serve at once or spoon into a shallow pan and place in freezer until semi-firm, but not hard-frozen, about 2 hours. If frozen in pan, spoon into serving dishes. Garnish with lemon twists, if you wish.

AVOCADO OMELET

This is a colorful omelet that makes a most satisfying luncheon entrée.

Makes 2 large omelets (4 servings).

¼ cup chopped green pepper
¼ cup chopped green onions
5 tablespoons butter or margarine
1 ripe tomato, peeled, seeded and chopped
¼ teaspoon Italian herb seasoning mix
¼ teaspoon salt
1 large avocado
1 tablespoon lemon juice
8 eggs
½ teaspoon salt
⅛ teaspoon pepper
¼ cup water

1. Sauté pepper and onions in 1 tablespoon of the butter in a small skillet until soft. Stir in tomato, Italian seasoning and ¼ teaspoon salt. Cook and stir until most of the liquid has evaporated; remove from heat.
2. Halve avocado; pit; peel. Sprinkle with lemon juice, then chop coarsely. Stir into tomato mixture.
3. Beat eggs with salt, pepper and water in a medium-size bowl until foamy. For each omelet: Heat 2 tablespoons of the butter in a large skillet until foamy-hot. Ladle half of the beaten egg mixture into the skillet. Stir the eggs rapidly with the flat of a fork, while shaking the skillet back and forth over the heat. Stir just until liquid sets, then cook 15 seconds longer.
4. Fold ⅓ of omelet toward center, then roll out onto serving plate. Omelet can be filled with ½ of the avocado filling just before rolling, or you can slash the rolled omelet lengthwise and spoon the filling into the cavity. Keep omelet warm in a very slow oven (275°) until other is made. Serve at once.

AVOCADO HALVES WITH TUNA SALAD

Warm cheese biscuits and a frosty fruit sherbet are good go-withs.

Makes 6 servings.

1 can (9¼ ounces) tuna, drained
1 medium-size onion, minced (½ cup)
1 clove garlic, mashed
1 cucumber, pared and diced
6 pimiento-stuffed green olives, chopped
1 teaspoon salt
⅓ cup mayonnaise or salad dressing
¼ cup light cream or half-and-half
3 large avocados
Lemon juice

1. Flake tuna into a medium-size bowl. Add onion, garlic, cucumber, olives and salt; toss lightly. Combine mayonnaise and cream in a small bowl; stir until smooth. Pour over tuna salad; toss just until mixed. Chill until serving time.
2. Halve avocados; remove pits. Brush cut surfaces with lemon juice to prevent darkening. Spoon tuna mixture into avocado cavities. Place filled avocado halves on plates. Garnish with a sprig of watercress, if you wish.

AVOCADO SOUP

Creamy and smooth, this pale green soup is equally good served hot or cold. It can be made a day ahead.

Makes about 6 servings.

2 medium-size avocados
¾ cup light cream or half-and-half
2 tablespoons minced onion
1 teaspoon lemon juice
½ teaspoon salt
3 cups chicken broth
2 tablespoons dry sherry
¼ cup toasted sliced almonds

1. Halve avocados; pit; peel. Cut into chunks and whirl in container of electric blender with some of the cream until smooth; pour into medium-size bowl. Add onion, lemon juice, salt and remaining cream.
2. Heat chicken broth to boiling in a large saucepan; lower heat. Stir in sherry and simmer mixture 2 minutes to blend flavors.
3. Stir avocado mixture into hot broth. (Do not heat over high heat or for too long a time, or the avocados will become bitter.) Remove from heat. Pour into soup bowls and sprinkle with almonds. Garnish with avocado slices, if you wish.

BABA AU RHUM A rich, yeast-leavened cake soaked in rum syrup, often baked in cylindrical molds.

BABA GHANOUSH A puree of eggplant seasoned with garlic, lemon juice and tahina (sesame) paste, then garnished with mint or pomegranate seeds. Arab in origin, it's served as an appetizer. See also **EGGPLANT**.

BACON Bacon is made by curing the belly side or loin of pork in dry salt or salt-sugar brine. Afterwards, the bacon is hung over smoldering wood dust to acquire a smoky taste. Each packer has his own recipe for curing and smoking and it's only by trying different brands that you learn which you prefer.
Buying and Storing: Buy the type of bacon that will fit your needs. *Regular sliced bacon* is available in 8-, 12- and 16-ounce vacuum-sealed packages. *Thick sliced bacon* is sold in 1-, 1½- and 2-pound packages. Use regular or thick slices where appearance is important such as for breakfast, in sandwiches or as a garnish. *Ends and Pieces* are money savers and can be used to flavor casseroles, soups and stews. They're sold in bulk packages or boxes. *Slab bacon* usually costs less than ready-sliced bacon. It's sold by the piece and can be sliced by the butcher or by yourself at home. *Bacon squares* are cut from the jowl of pigs. They are cured and smoked like bacon. Use this thrifty cut for seasoning food. *Salt pork* is dry salt or brine-cured pork or pork fat. It's not smoked. Use it like bacon for seasoning. *Canadian-style bacon* is boneless pork loin, cured and smoked. It tastes more like ham, and is sold sliced or by the piece. Slices are delicious for breakfast or sandwiches. Today you will also find *fabricated bacon strips* made from vegetable protein or ground meat. They are ideal for special diets.

Keep bacon in its original wrapper in the refrigerator. Freezing bacon is not recommended for long periods of time because the salt draws out the moisture and affects the flavor. Tip: bacon slices tear easily when cold, so take bacon out of the refrigerator 10 minutes before cooking. If you forget, try this trick: Place a rubber spatula under one end of a slice then run it slowly between slices to separate.
How to Cook: Perfectly cooked bacon should be crisp, not brittle. You can pan-fry, bake, broil or microwave bacon. To pan fry, place slices in a cold skillet. No need to separate them; they'll fall apart as they cook. Cook slowly, turning often until crisp and brown. Drain on paper toweling. To bake, place slices on a rack in a shallow pan with fat edge of one slice overlapping lean of next. Bake in a hot oven (400°) 12 to 15 minutes or until crisp. No need to turn slices; the perfect way to cook bacon for a crowd. To broil, arrange slices as for baking, but use rack in broiler pan. Broil about 4 inches from heat, turning once, 2 to 3 minutes on each side or until crisp. To microwave, place several layers of paper toweling on oven floor, paper or microwave-proof plate. Place up to 6 bacon slices on toweling; cover with more toweling. Microwave on high power 45 seconds to 1 minute per slice. Let stand 5 minutes. For more than 6 slices, microwave 30 to 45 seconds per slice. Bacon will appear underdone when first removed from oven but upon standing it will be brown and crisp.

•●•

BAGNA CAUDA Translated "hot bath," bagna cauda is an Italian sauce flavored with anchovies and garlic. It is served over cooked vegetables, fish or meats, or as a dip for bread sticks and raw vegetables.

BAGNA CAUDA

Here's a party dip with pizzazz.

Makes 8 servings.

- **3 cups heavy cream**
- **6 tablespoons (3/4 stick) unsalted butter**
- **1 can (2 ounces) anchovy fillets, drained and mashed**
- **1 clove garlic, minced**
- **2 cucumbers, pared, cut into bite-size sticks**
- **2 heads fennel, washed, trimmed and cut into slender wedges**
- **1 bunch young green onions, cut into 3-inch lengths**
- **1/2 pint cherry tomatoes**
- **1/2 pound very fresh mushrooms, quartered—if large, or halved, leave stems on**
- **Italian bread sticks or 1 loaf crusty Italian bread, cubed**

1. Simmer heavy cream in a small saucepan, stirring occasionally, until reduced to half its volume (1½ cups). This will take about 20 minutes.
2. Melt butter in a skillet; add anchovies and garlic; cook 2 minutes, stirring often. Stir in hot cream. Pour into chafing dish. Keep warm over low heat while dipping vegetables or bread.
3. Arrange vegetables and bread on tray around chafing dish.

•●•

BAKLAVA A multi-layered, sweet pastry of honey and nuts from Middle Eastern cuisines. Each layer of phyllo, the paper-thin pastry, is buttered and then sprinkled with sugared-and-spiced ground nuts. The pastry is cut into diamond shapes to serve.

BAKLAVA

Bake nuts at 350° for 10 minutes.
Bake at 325° for 50 minutes.
Makes about 3½ dozen pieces.

- **3 cups walnuts (about 3/4 pound)**
- **1/2 cup sugar**
- **1½ teaspoons ground cinnamon**
- **1 package (16 ounces) phyllo or strudel pastry leaves**
- **1/2 cup (1 stick) unsalted butter or margarine, melted**
- **1 tablespoon water**
- **Honey Syrup *(recipe follows)***

1. Place walnuts on a 15½ × 10½ × 1-inch jelly-roll pan; toast in a moderate oven (350°) for 10 minutes. Whirl walnuts, while still warm, ½ cup at a time, in container of electric blender until finely ground. (You may use a food grinder or food processor, if you wish.) Remove ground walnuts to a medium-size bowl. Repeat this procedure until all of the walnuts are ground. Mix in the sugar and ground cinnamon; set aside.
2. Brush bottom of a 13 × 9 × 2-inch baking pan with melted butter. Fold two phyllo leaves in half; place on the bottom of pan; brush with butter. Place two more folded leaves in pan; brush with butter. (Keep rest of pastry leaves covered with a clean damp kitchen towel to prevent drying out.)
3. Sprinkle top with ½ cup nut mixture. Add two more folded leaves; brush with butter.
4. Repeat step 3 five more times. Stack remaining leaves, brushing every other one. Brush top leaf with remaining butter; sprinkle with the 1 tablespoon water.
5. With a sharp knife, mark off the Baklava. Cut through the top layer of the phyllo only, making 5 lengthwise cuts, 1½ inches apart (you will have 6 equal strips). Then cut diagonally again at 1½-inch intervals, making diamonds (9 strips).
6. Bake in a slow oven (325°) for 50 minutes, or until top is golden. Remove pan to wire rack. Cut all the way through the diamonds, separating slightly. Pour cooled Honey Syrup over. Cool thoroughly in pan on rack. Cover with foil; let stand at room temperature overnight for syrup to be absorbed. Baklava will keep in refrigerator up to 2 weeks.

HONEY SYRUP

Makes 2 cups.

- **1 small lemon**
- **1 cup sugar**
- **1 cup water**
- **1 two-inch piece stick cinnamon**
- **2 whole cloves**
- **1 cup honey**
- **1 tablespoon brandy (optional)**

1. Grate the rind from the lemon (the thin, yellow skin only) and reserve. Squeeze out 1½ teaspoons lemon juice into a small cup; set aside.
2. Place lemon rind, sugar, water, cinnamon stick and cloves in a heavy medium-size saucepan. Bring to boiling; lower heat; continue cooking, without stirring, 25 minutes, or until mixture is syrupy (230° on a candy thermometer).
3. Stir in honey; pour through strainer into a 2-cup measure. Stir in reserved lemon juice and brandy. Cool.

•●•

BAMBOO SHOOT An Oriental vegetable, bamboo shoots come from the young shoots of an edible variety of the bamboo plant. The hard sheaths covering the shoots are removed to reveal a soft, creamy-white, fleshy core. Bamboo shoots are boiled and cut into pieces or slices. They are canned in water or brine and exported from the Far East to our markets. In some markets you'll find a distinction made between winter and spring bamboo shoots. The winter shoots are tastier and thus more expensive. Spring shoots are tougher, darker, and cheaper. Store unused bamboo shoots, covered with water, in a jar in the refrigerator.

BANANA First brought to the New World by Spaniards, bananas flourished in the lands bordering the Caribbean Sea. From there, the first bananas were brought to the United States more than 150 years ago. Americans considered them a luxury fruit. Now, bananas are very popular, and available year round.

Bananas are considered a staple food in the countries where they are grown. There are numerous varieties, ranging in color from the familiar golden yellow to red to the green plantain. Plantains must be cooked before they are palatable. They are served as a starchy vegetable.

Buying and Storing: Bananas are harvested green and are shipped year-round to our markets. Firm green bananas are excellent when cooked and served as a vegetable. As a banana ripens, the green peel changes to yellow and the fruit becomes soft. Its starch changes to sugar and it develops a fruity aroma. Use the ripe banana in salads, or for desserts.

Buy firm, unblemished fruit. Keep at room temperature. If bananas ripen before you are able to use them, they may be refrigerated. The cold temperature will slow down ripening for several days. Although the peel will turn dark, the fruit is still edible. You can freeze the mashed pulp in airtight containers with lemon juice or ascorbic-acid mixture added.

Banana Nutrition: A six-inch banana has 85 calories. It's a good source of potassium, thiamin, riboflavin, niacin and vitamins A and C.

Banana Math
1 pound=3 medium-size bananas
1 medium banana=⅔ cup sliced or ½ cup diced or ⅓ cup mashed

BANANA NUT BREAD

Bake at 325° for 1 hour, 20 minutes.
Makes 1 loaf.

2½ cups *sifted* all-purpose flour
3 teaspoons baking powder
½ teaspoon salt
¼ teaspoon baking soda
½ cup (1 stick) butter or margarine
1 cup sugar
3 eggs
3 medium-size ripe bananas, peeled and mashed (1 cup)
¼ cup wheat germ
½ cup finely chopped walnuts
½ cup raisins, chopped

1. Sift flour, baking powder, salt and baking soda onto wax paper. Grease a 9×5×3-inch loaf pan; line bottom with wax paper; grease paper.
2. Beat butter, sugar and eggs in a large bowl until light and fluffy; stir in bananas. Preheat oven to 325°.
3. Stir in flour mixture; fold in wheat germ, walnuts and raisins. Pour into prepared pan.
4. Bake in a preheated slow oven (325°) for 1 hour and 20 minutes, or until a wooden pick inserted near the center comes out clean. Cool in pan on a wire rack 10 minutes. Loosen around edges with knife; turn out onto rack; peel off wax paper. Let cool completely. Wrap in aluminum foil and store overnight for easier slicing.

BANANA CREAM PIE

Creamy-smooth, and oh, so delicious!
Makes one 9-inch pie.

½ package piecrust mix
⅔ cup sugar
3 tablespoons flour
2 tablespoons cornstarch
¼ teaspoon salt
3 cups milk
3 eggs
2 teaspoons vanilla
3 medium-size ripe bananas
1 cup heavy cream

1. Prepare piecrust mix following label directions for a baked pastry shell.
2. Combine sugar, flour, cornstarch and salt in a large saucepan. Stir in milk slowly.
3. Cook, stirring constantly, over moderate heat, until mixture thickens and bubbles. Continue cooking and stirring until mixture is very thick, about 6 minutes longer.
4. Beat eggs in a medium-size bowl until frothy. Stir in half of the cooked mixture until blended. Return to saucepan, blending in mixture. Cook 2 minutes more over low heat, stirring constantly.
5. Remove from heat; stir in vanilla. Place a piece of plastic wrap directly on surface; cool.
6. Peel and slice bananas into pie shell. Pour cooled cream filling over bananas; chill several hours. Whip cream in a medium-size bowl until stiff. Spoon over top of pie.

BANANA DESSERT CRÊPES

Try this recipe on your family first, then put it on the menu for your next dinner party.
Makes 6 servings.

Crêpes:
½ cup *sifted* all-purpose flour
1 tablespoon sugar
⅛ teaspoon salt
2 eggs
¾ cup milk
1 tablespoon butter, melted

Orange Sauce:
¼ cup (½ stick) butter or margarine
⅓ cup sugar
2 teaspoons grated orange rind
⅓ cup orange juice
3 small bananas
2 tablespoons rum

1. Make Crêpes: Combine flour, sugar, salt, eggs and milk in a medium-size bowl; beat with rotary beater until smooth. Beat in the 1 tablespoon butter. Let stand 20 minutes.
2. Slowly heat 7-inch skillet or crêpe pan until a drop of water sizzles when dropped on surface. Butter skillet lightly for the first few crêpes.
3. Pour batter, 2 tablespoons for each crêpe, into heated skillet; quickly rotate skillet to spread batter evenly. Cook over medium heat until lightly browned; turn and brown other side. Remove to plate. Cool, then fold in quarters.
4. Make Sauce: Combine butter, sugar, orange rind and orange juice in a large chafing dish or skillet; bring to boiling. Peel bananas; cut in quarters lengthwise; add to skillet; heat 1 minute. Add crêpes and heat, spooning sauce over. Heat rum in a small saucepan; ignite; pour over crêpes. Serve 2 crêpes and 2 pieces of banana per serving.

BANANAS FOSTER

Makes 4 servings.

½ cup firmly packed brown sugar
¼ cup (½ stick) butter or margarine
4 ripe bananas, peeled and quartered
Dash of ground cinnamon
½ cup light rum
¼ cup banana liqueur
1 pint vanilla ice cream

1. Melt brown sugar and butter or margarine in a chafing dish or skillet, stirring often.
2. Add bananas and sauté just until soft (don't overcook). Sprinkle cinnamon over bananas.
3. Heat rum and banana liqueur in a small saucepan. Pour over bananas, *but do not stir into sauce.* Carefully light liquor in chafing dish and keep spooning sauce over bananas till flames die.
4. Scoop ice cream into 4 large dessert dishes. Spoon bananas and sauce over and serve immediately.

BARBECUE Everything from frankfurters to turkey and vegetables tastes better when cooked over the coals. To barbecue is to cook foods over an open fire or gas grill. The most popular way is to use charcoal briquets.

Grilling Tips

Proper grilling techniques are important for succulent, crusty, charcoal-flavored — not smothered — barbecued food. Here are a dozen pointers for no-fail, no-burn barbecues.

- Start a charcoal fire at least 30 to 40 minutes before you start to cook, to allow the coals to burn and become covered with a gray ash. The heat will be radiant and will cook the food gradually without burning.
- For easy clean-up, line the fire pan of the grill with heavy-duty foil.
- Heap the charcoal in the center of the grill or around the drip pan (if you're using one) and set aflame.
- To start the fire, use charcoal starter or an electric starter. Chemical charcoal starter may cause "off" flavors in foods, but the electric starter imparts no odor.
- When the coals are hot, separate them into an even layer on the bottom of the grill. To add coals, start them burning in another pan and transfer them to the grill when they are gray.
- When grilling fatty foods, make a drip pan of foil and place directly under food to prevent fat flare-ups.
- To maintain an even temperature, place the grill in a sheltered place away from drafts. On a windy day, cover the grill with a hood or a tent of foil.
- Keep a sprinkler bottle of water handy for dousing occasional flames.
- When grilling foods that need slow cooking, set the grill rack at its highest position and lower it during cooking as the coals get cooler.
- When you use a gas grill, the same principles apply. Preheat the grill to allow the ceramic element to become radiantly hot. Use marinades and barbecue sauces that contain as little sugar as possible, but if you have a favorite sweet sauce, keep the grill rack as high as possible, turn foods every five minutes and brush with sauce every time food is turned. Use tongs for turning to prevent piercing food and releasing juices.
- If any marinade or basting sauce remains, heat it in a saucepan on the grill rack and serve it.
- The last glowing embers can be used to keep coffee hot, toast marshmallows or pound cake, heat fudge or butter-pecan sauce for ice cream, warm cookies, rolls, apple pie or grill orange or pineapple slices.

Cooking Hints

- If your firebox is not adjustable, cook food on hinged grill that you can raise and lower manually.
- Brush grill with fat or oil or use vegetable cooking spray just before cooking to prevent food from sticking.
- When wrapping food to be cooked in aluminum foil, place the shiny side of the foil toward the food.
- Trim all excess fat from meat to prevent drippings from flaring up.
- Score meats such as steaks or chops at the edges to prevent curling.
- Salt meat after juices have been sealed in by searing.
- Sprinkle the charcoal with fresh herbs such as marjoram, rosemary, thyme or mint, or dried herbs such as bay leaves or fennel, soaked in water, to give the grilled meat a subtle flavor.
- To make hamburgers hold together while cooking, add one egg and ¼ cup bread crumbs to each pound of meat. Or broil hamburgers on foil: Punch holes in the foil at 2-inch intervals to let the fat drip down and the smoke flavor the meat.
- When placing meat on a spit for rotisserie cooking, be sure to balance it properly so it will rotate evenly.

Safety Tips

- Don't use kerosene to start a fire. Besides being dangerous, it will make the food taste of kerosene.
- Never use gasoline to start a fire—you can end up in the hospital.
- Do not add more liquid starter once the charcoal has ignited—it can flare up dramatically.
- Keep children and pets away from the grill while lighting and cooking.
- Keep the grill away from where people are sitting so a change in wind won't blow smoke or sparks on them.
- Wear clothes without dangling scarves, strings or shirttails.
- Use your grill in a well-ventilated area—not in your garage.
- Grill in an indoor fireplace only if it has a good draft.

Temperature Guide for Grilling

TESTING BY: Thermometer

Low
about 300°

Medium
about 350°

Hot
about 400°

TESTING BY: Hand*

Low
4-5 seconds

Medium
3-4 seconds

Hot
less than 3 seconds

**The length of time you can hold your hand over the coals before you have to remove it determines the distance your grill should be from the coals.*

GRILLED KNOCKWURST WITH FRUIT GLAZE

Grill 10 to 15 minutes.
Makes 4 servings.

6 tablespoons grape jelly
3 tablespoons chili sauce
1 tablespoon prepared mustard
¼ teaspoon ground cloves
1 pound knockwurst, Polish sausage or frankfurters, scored

1. Heat jelly, chili sauce, mustard and cloves in small saucepan, stirring occasionally, just until smooth.
2. Grill sausages about 5 inches from grayed coals, brushing often with glaze, just until heated through, 10 to 15 minutes.

Pictured opposite: Banana Nut Bread, page 37

STUFFED TWIN CHICKENS

Roast on rotisserie for 1 hour and 45 minutes.
Makes 8 servings.

- **1 medium-size zucchini, shredded (1 cup)**
- **2 tablespoons butter or margarine**
- **1½ cups water**
- **1 package (6½ ounces) stuffing mix with rice**
- **¾ cup shredded Swiss cheese**
- **2 broiler-fryers (2 to 2½ pounds each)**
- **1 teaspoon salt**
- **Lemon-Herb Butter Baste *(recipe follows)***

1. Sauté zucchini in butter in a large saucepan 5 minutes; add water and seasonings from stuffing mix; bring to boiling. Remove from heat. Add stuffing crumbs; mix lightly with fork until moist. Let stand to cool slightly, 15 minutes; fold in cheese.
2. Wash chickens; pat dry with paper toweling. Rub inside and out with salt. Lightly stuff body and neck cavities with stuffing. Skewer neck skin to body; securely close body cavity; tie legs and wings tightly to body.
3. Place chickens on rotisserie spit and roast 1 hour and 45 minutes, brushing every 15 minutes with Lemon-Herb Butter Baste, until chickens are browned and tender.

Note: A roasting chicken (4 to 4½ pounds) can be substituted for broiler-fryers. Increase roasting time about 30 minutes. Extra stuffing can be wrapped in foil and heated on grill.

Lemon-Herb Butter Baste: Melt 3 tablespoons butter or margarine in a small saucepan; add 1 teaspoon grated lemon rind, 2 tablespoons lemon juice, 1 teaspoon aromatic bitters and ½ teaspoon leaf basil.

MARINATED BEEF ROUND

Roast on rotisserie for 1½ hours.
Makes 12 servings.

- **1 eye-round or top round roast (about 4 pounds and 4 inches in diameter)**
- **1 cup red wine**
- **⅓ cup red wine vinegar**
- **1 large onion, chopped (1 cup)**
- **2 envelopes instant beef broth**
- **1 teaspoon Italian herb seasoning mix**
- **1 teaspoon salt**
- **½ teaspoon coarse black pepper**
- **2 tablespoons butter or margarine**
- **¼ cup finely chopped parsley**
- **2 cloves garlic, finely chopped**

1. Pierce meat deeply with a fork for flavors to penetrate. Place in a plastic bag in a large bowl.
2. Combine wine, vinegar, onion, beef broth, herbs, salt and pepper; pour over meat in plastic bag; tie closed. Marinate in refrigerator for 24 to 48 hours, turning occasionally.
3. Remove meat from marinade; make deep incisions in meat with the tip of a knife. Mix butter, parsley and garlic to a smooth paste; push mixture into incisions. Tie roast with string every two inches.
4. Insert spit lengthwise through center of meat. Fasten with holding forks so it won't slip. Insert meat thermometer in thickest part of meat.
5. Roast over grayed coals, basting with marinade every 20 minutes, 1 hour and 30 minutes or until thermometer registers 140° for rare. Remove spit and allow roast to rest 15 minutes, covered loosely with aluminum foil.

SAVORY GRILLED SHORT RIBS

Grill for about 1 hour.
Makes 6 servings.

- **4 pounds beef short ribs, cut into serving-size pieces**
- **1 teaspoon salt**
- **½ teaspoon pepper**
- **½ cup catsup**
- **1 cup beer**
- **¼ cup bottled steak sauce**

1. Rub meat with salt and pepper. Roast ribs 6 inches from grayed coals 30 minutes, turning often.
2. Combine catsup, beer and steak sauce in a small saucepan; bring to boiling. Brush part over ribs; continue to roast and brush often with beer baste 30 minutes more or until meat is medium rare or done to your taste. Serve ribs with any remaining baste as a sauce.

ITALIAN FIESTA SAUSAGES

Grill 20 to 30 minutes.
Makes 4 servings.

- **1½ pounds Italian-style sausages, sweet or hot (8 to 10 sausages)**
- **2 medium-size zucchini, split lengthwise, then cut in half**
- **2 small red peppers, quartered and seeded**
- **1 small onion, peeled and halved**
- **½ cup Italian or oil and vinegar salad dressing**

1. Alternate sausages, zucchini and peppers on skewers; thread ½ onion on the end of each skewer; brush generously with salad dressing.
2. Grill about 5 inches from heat over grayed coals, turning skewers often and brushing with dressing, 20 minutes or until sausages are cooked through.

SAUSAGE AND CHICKEN LIVERS EN BROCHETTE

Grill 6 to 8 minutes.
Makes 4 servings.

- **½ pound chicken livers, washed and halved**
- **1 package (8 ounces) brown-and-serve sausage, cut in half**
- **3 bacon slices, cut in 1½-inch pieces**
- **1 red cooking apple, quartered, cored and cut into chunks**
- **1 bunch green onions, cut into 2-inch pieces**
- **2 tablespoons soy sauce**
- **2 tablespoons Worcestershire sauce**
- **1 tablespoon lemon juice**
- **¼ teaspoon leaf thyme, crumbled**

1. Alternate pieces of liver, sausage, bacon, apple and onion on skewers.
2. Combine soy and Worcestershire sauces, lemon juice and thyme in a small cup.
3. Place skewers on grill 5 to 6 inches over grayed coals for 6 to 8 minutes or until cooked through. Turn and brush often with soy sauce mixture. Serve with hot cooked rice, if you wish.

BARBECUED TURKEY LEGS

Grill 1 hour and 45 minutes.
Makes 6 servings.

- **2 packages ($2\frac{1}{2}$ pounds each) fresh or frozen turkey legs**
- **1 container (8 ounces) plain yogurt**
- **1 envelope garlic-flavored salad-dressing mix**
- **1 tablespoon lemon juice**

1. Thaw turkey legs if frozen; dry with paper toweling. Combine yogurt, salad-dressing mix and lemon juice in shallow dish large enough to hold legs in one layer. Brush legs with yogurt mixture; cover; refrigerate overnight.
2. Wrap legs in individual foil packets, reserving yogurt. Place on grill 5 to 6 inches from grayed coals, 1 hour.
3. Unwrap and place legs on grill to brown. Brush with reserved yogurt, turning often.
4. Continue to grill 45 minutes until juices run clear when pierced with fork. Heat any remaining marinade to serve with turkey.

SWEET CORN ON THE COB

Grilling corn in its own husk is a great flavor saver.

Roast 15 to 25 minutes.
Makes 8 servings.

- **8 ears fresh corn**
- **Softened butter or margarine**
- **Salt**
- **Pepper**

1. To roast corn in husks, remove only outer husks; fold back inner ones, being careful not to split them; remove silks. Spread corn with butter; sprinkle with salt and pepper. Pull husks back up over ears; tie tips with string to keep corn covered and moist.
2. To roast corn in aluminum foil, husk and remove silks; spread with butter and season with salt and pepper. Wrap well in heavy-duty or double-thick regular aluminum foil.
3. Place corn on grill over gray coals. Roast 15 to 25 minutes, turning several times to grill evenly.

Overleaf: Sausage and Chicken Livers en Brochette, page 40; Italian Fiesta Sausages, page 40; Grilled Knockwurst with Fruit Glaze, page 39

HERBED GARLIC AND ONION BREAD

You can make the herb butter ahead of time and refrigerate.

Grill about 15 minutes.
Makes 8 servings.

- **$\frac{1}{2}$ cup (1 stick) butter or margarine**
- **1 clove garlic, finely chopped**
- **2 tablespoons instant minced onion**
- **$\frac{1}{4}$ teaspoon leaf marjoram, crumbled**
- **$\frac{1}{4}$ teaspoon leaf thyme, crumbled**
- **1 loaf French or Italian bread, 12 to 14 inches long**

1. Combine butter, garlic, onion, marjoram and thyme in bowl until well mixed.
2. Cut bread into 1-inch-thick slices, but don't cut all the way through bottom crust. Spread herb butter on cut surface of slices. Wrap loaf in heavy-duty or double-thick regular aluminum foil.
3. Place bread on grill; grill until heated through, about 15 minutes. Unwrap and break into slices to serve.

Note: Bread can be heated in an oven. Bake bread in a preheated hot oven (400°)for 15 minutes.

BARLEY Like wheat, barley is a member of the grass family and one of the earliest cultivated grains. At one time, barley was used extensively in making bread, but its low gluten content resulted in a heavy loaf. So, barley has given way in breadmaking to wheat flour, which is higher in protein as well as in gluten.

Barley makes a tasty addition to hearty soups and stews. But, today, most of the world's barley goes into the production of beer and scotch whiskey.

Buying and Storing: The barley you find in the market is labeled "pearl" barley, which means that the grain has been freed of its hull by a special polishing method. Store in the cupboard in airtight containers.

BEEF AND BARLEY SOUP

Makes 6 servings.

- **3 pounds meaty cross-cut beef shank or neck**
- **$\frac{1}{4}$ cup all-purpose flour**
- **$\frac{1}{4}$ cup vegetable oil**
- **$\frac{3}{4}$ cup pearl barley**
- **2 carrots, cut into quarters lengthwise**
- **1 medium-size onion, thinly sliced**
- **$\frac{1}{2}$ cup chopped fresh parsley**
- **1 bay leaf**
- **2 teaspoons salt**
- **$\frac{1}{2}$ teaspoon pepper**
- **$\frac{1}{2}$ teaspoon leaf thyme, crumbled**
- **$\frac{1}{2}$ teaspoon leaf savory, crumbled**
- **2 cans ($13\frac{3}{4}$ ounces each) beef broth**

1. Dredge meat with flour. Brown in oil on all sides in large kettle.
2. Combine meat with barley, carrots, onion, parsley, bay leaf, salt, pepper, thyme, savory and beef broth in the kettle.
3. Cover and cook on low heat for 2 hours or until beef and barley are tender. Remove meat; discard bones and dice meat. Return to soup.
4. Taste for seasoning; add additional salt or thyme, if you wish.

BASIL There are many varieties of this fragrant, annual herb, but only a few are cultivated for culinary and ornamental purposes. Purple basil is grown in home gardens for its decorative foliage. Sweet basil, a culinary variety, grows in many temperate areas. A native of the Middle East, the Mediterranean and India, sweet basil has a spicy, clove-like flavor that complements eggs, cheese, tomatoes, fish and poultry. Basil is available fresh during the summer and is dried for year-round use. You can preserve fresh leaves by freezing them, or by packing them in a jar of olive oil and refrigerating. Try drying fresh leaves in the microwave. Basil is used extensively to make a delicious sauce called *pesto* in Genoa or *pistou* in Provence.

PESTO GENOVESE

Sweet basil leaves give this pesto sauce its unique flavor and aroma. Basil is great with other pastas too!

Makes 6 servings.

- **1 cup olive or vegetable oil**
- **2 cloves garlic, crushed**
- **3 tablespoons pine nuts *(pignoli)***
- **2 cups firmly packed fresh basil leaves***
- **1 teaspoon salt**
- **¼ teaspoon pepper**
- **1 cup freshly grated Parmesan cheese**
- **1 package (16 ounces) linguini**

1. Place oil and garlic in electric blender container; cover; blend on high speed until smooth. With blades spinning, remove inner cap of cover, gradually add pine nuts, blending until smooth. Add basil leaves, a few at a time, until well-blended. Add salt and pepper, then gradually add Parmesan cheese, stopping blender to stir down mixture with a thin rubber spatula.
2. Cook linguini following label directions. Reserve ½ cup of the cooking liquid, then drain off remaining cooking liquid. Return linguini to kettle; toss with reserved cooking liquid. Pour onto a large heated platter; pour pesto sauce over and toss with two forks until evenly blended. Serve with additional grated Parmesan, if you wish.

**When substituting dried leaf basil for fresh: Crumble 2 teaspoons basil into the oil. Let stand 15 minutes to bring out the flavor. Then add 2 cups parsley clusters (not stems) for fresh green color.*

Note: If you should reheat the linguini and pesto, the oil will separate a little, but that will not affect the taste.

BASS A number of unrelated fresh and salt water fish are called bass. The widely distributed largemouth and smallmouth bass are not true bass but members of the sunfish family. An example of a true bass is the black sea bass.

BAVARIAN CREAM Originally called *bavarois* or *fromage bavarois*, Bavarian cream is basically a gelatin dessert blended with egg custard and whipped cream. It can be flavored in a number of ways: with fruits, such as strawberries, peaches or lemons or with chocolate, vanilla or a liqueur. Bavarian creams are usually molded in fancy shapes, then served with a sauce.

RAINBOW BAVARIAN CREAM

Yellow, green and white layers create such a showy effect for so little effort.

Makes 6 to 8 servings.

- **4 eggs, separated**
- **¾ cup sugar**
- **1 cup water**
- **1 envelope unflavored gelatin**
- **¼ cup lemon juice**
- **1 teaspoon vanilla**
- **1 cup heavy cream**
- **Yellow and green food colorings**

1. Beat egg yolks slightly in the top of a double boiler; stir in ¼ cup of the sugar and water; sprinkle gelatin over top; let stand several minutes to soften gelatin.
2. Cook, stirring constantly, over simmering water 10 minutes, or until gelatin dissolves and mixture coats a spoon; remove from heat. Stir in lemon juice and vanilla. Strain into a large bowl.
3. Set bowl in a pan of ice and water to speed setting. Chill, stirring often, just until mixture is as thick as unbeaten egg white.
4. While gelatin mixture chills, beat egg whites in a large bowl until foamy-white and double in volume; beat in remaining ½ cup sugar, 1 tablespoon at a time, until sugar dissolves completely and meringue forms stiff peaks. Beat cream until stiff in a small bowl.
5. Fold whipped cream, then meringue into thickened gelatin mixture until no streaks of white remain; remove from ice and water. Spoon 1 cup into a deep 6-cup mold; set mold in ice and water; chill until not quite firm. Tint remaining mixture in bowl pale yellow with food coloring; spoon 2 cups into mold; chill again. Tint remaining mixture pale green with food coloring; spoon over yellow layer; remove from ice and water. Chill at least 4 hours or overnight.
6. When ready to serve, run a sharp thin-blade knife around top of dessert, then dip mold *very quickly* in and out of a pan of hot water. Cover with a serving plate; turn upside down; gently lift off mold. Cut in wedges; serve with your favorite lemon sauce, if you wish.

STRAWBERRY YOGURT BAVARIAN

Chill this innovative version of the popular Bavarian cream in a large, pretty mold and serve at a luncheon or dinner party.

Makes 10 to 12 servings.

- **2 envelopes unflavored gelatin**
- **½ cup cold water**
- **8 tablespoons sugar**
- **4 eggs, separated**
- **¼ teaspoon salt**
- **2 packages (10 ounces each) frozen sliced strawberries, thawed**
- **2 tablespoons lemon juice**
- **2 containers (8 ounces each) plain yogurt**

1. Sprinkle gelatin over water in a medium-size saucepan to soften. Add 6 tablespoons of the sugar, egg yolks, which have been lightly beaten, salt and strawberries.
2. Cook over low heat, stirring constantly, until gelatin is dissolved and mixture coats a spoon, about 8 minutes.
3. Remove from heat and add lemon juice and yogurt. Mix well and turn into a large bowl; chill until mixture begins to thicken.
4. Beat egg whites in a large bowl until foamy. Add remaining 2 tablespoons sugar and beat until stiff. Fold into strawberry-yogurt mixture and spoon into a 2-quart mold.
5. Cover; chill until firm, at least 4 hours, or overnight.
6. When ready to serve, loosen edges of mold with a knife, dip mold in hot water, turn out on a chilled serving plate. Garnish with whipped cream or fresh strawberries and toasted almonds, if you wish.

CAFÉ CREAM ROYALE

Such a lusciously rich way to enjoy coffee and cream.
Makes 8 to 10 servings.

6 eggs, separated
¾ cup sugar
Dash salt
2 cups warm freshly brewed coffee
2 envelopes unflavored gelatin
3 tablespoons light rum
1 cup heavy cream

1. Beat egg yolks slightly in the top of a double boiler; stir in ¼ cup of the sugar, salt and coffee; sprinkle gelatin over top; let stand several minutes to soften gelatin.
2. Cook, stirring constantly, over simmering water 10 minutes, or until gelatin dissolves and mixture coats a spoon; remove from heat. Strain into a large bowl; stir in rum.
3. Place bowl in a pan of ice and water to speed setting. Chill, stirring often, just until as thick as unbeaten egg white.
4. While gelatin mixture chills, beat egg whites in a large bowl until foamy-white and double in volume; beat in remaining ½ cup sugar, 1 tablespoon at a time, until sugar dissolves completely and meringue forms stiff peaks. Beat cream until stiff in a small bowl.
5. Fold whipped cream, then meringue into thickened gelatin mixture until no streaks of white remain. Spoon into a 2-quart mold. Chill at least 6 hours, or overnight.
6. When ready to serve, run a sharp, thin knife blade around top of dessert, then dip mold *very quickly* in and out of a pan of hot water. Cover with a serving plate; turn upside down; gently lift off mold.

•●•

BAY LEAF One of the best known culinary herbs. The bay leaf is the leaf of the laurel tree. It is sometimes called sweet bay or Grecian laurel.

The bay leaf goes far back in history. In ancient Greek and Roman mythology, the laurel tree originated when the nymph Daphne was being pursued by Apollo and, in distress, she called to the gods to save her. The gods changed her into the laurel tree. Thereafter, the leaves were considered divine and used to make wreaths to crown conquerors, Olympic winners and poets. The word "baccalaureate" probably originated with the laurel crowning. "Bacca" meant berry and "laureate" meant laureled; thus "covered with berries of laurel. Use the fragrant leaves, fresh or dried, in stews, tomato sauces, soups, marinades and in *bouquet garni.*

BEANS Fresh, frozen, canned or dried, beans are versatile, tasty, economical and nutritious. Beans are the seeds of legume plants. They're loaded with protein, so with the addition of a little meat, cheese, eggs or grain, you up the protein value even more. Since the dawn of civilization, beans have been grown for food in many countries.

Kinds of Beans: (See also specific bean) *Green or snap beans* and wax beans are young pods with immature seeds. Pods and seeds are eaten. They are sold fresh, frozen or canned.

Fresh lima, either Baby or Fordhook, are the shelled, unripe seeds of the pods. Sold fresh in the pods or frozen or canned, shelled.

Fresh fava beans, blackeyed peas and cranberry beans in their pods are also found in some markets. Shell before cooking. Shelled *blackeyed peas,* also called beans, are available frozen, canned and dried.

Dried beans are mature or ripe seeds from the pods. They come in many varieties, including black or turtle beans, blackeyed peas, chick-peas (garbanzo beans), cranberry beans, lima, pinto, pink, red, red or white kidney beans, soybeans, Great Northern, Navy, pea, lentils, split or whole green or yellow peas and marrow beans.

Buying and Storing: Fresh green or wax beans are sold all year but the bulk of the crop appears from May to October. Select crisp, unblemished pods with small seeds. For limas, and other shelled fresh beans, choose well-filled unblemished pods. Refrigerate in plastic bags and use within 5 days. Dried beans are sold in pound packages. Keep them in a dry place; use within a year. Presoaked dried beans will keep 2 to 3 days in the refrigerator. Fully cooked beans will keep a week refrigerated, or 6 months in the freezer. To freeze, line a casserole with foil. Pour in the freshly cooked beans and let cool. Cover with foil; label and freeze. When frozen solid, remove from the casserole and return to the freezer. To reheat, remove foil from beans. Place beans in casserole and defrost overnight in the refrigerator or use the microwave. Bake in a moderate oven (350°) or microwave on high power until heated through. A number of fresh and dried beans are commercially frozen or canned. Buy only undented cans; keep in cool cupboard and use within 2 years. Buy only solidly frozen packages of beans; keep frozen until ready to use.

Cooking Beans: Wash green or wax beans; snap off stem ends. Leave whole or cut into pieces. Drop into a saucepan with 1 inch of boiling water. Cook covered just until tender, 3 to 5 minutes. Drain, season and serve. Canned beans are fully cooked; drain and use for salads or reheat and season. Frozen beans are partially cooked; cook in water or in the microwave according to package directions.

All varieties of dried beans with the exception of split peas and lentils are improved by soaking before cooking. Two methods can be used for soaking. Beans tend to hold their shape better with the long soak; place washed beans in a bowl with 2 to 3 times their volume of water (1 pound beans needs 4 to 6 cups); let stand 8 to 12 hours. To quick soak: bring water and beans to a boil; boil 2 minutes; cover pot and remove from heat; let stand 1 hour. The time required for cooking beans varies. It depends upon the variety and the length of time the beans have been stored. Check beans often as they begin to get tender so they don't get mushy. Cook at a gentle simmer to retain shape. If beans foam up during cooking, add a tablespoon of oil or fat to the water. Increase the cooking and soaking time in hard water areas and at high altitudes. If a recipe calls for tomatoes, lemon juice, vinegar or wine, add when beans are almost tender or acid will slow the softening process. Beans can be cooked in a crock pot, pressure cooker or in the microwave.

Bean Math

1 pound fresh green or wax beans=3 cups or 4 servings.
1 pound fresh limas in pods=⅔ cup shelled or about 1 serving.
1 pound dried beans=about 2 cups raw or 5 to 6 cups cooked.
1 can (16 ounces) beans=about 1⅔ cups drained
1 package (9 or 10 ounces) frozen beans=about 1½ cups

CURRIED LIMAS AND CHICKEN WINGS

A hearty, mildly seasoned casserole with peas and carrots.

Bake at 350° for 30 minutes.
Makes about 8 servings.

1 pound dried lima beans
8 cups water
8 chicken wings (about 1¼ pounds)
¼ cup (½ stick) butter or margarine
1 large onion, chopped
3 carrots, sliced (1½ cups)
2 teaspoons curry powder
¼ teaspoon ground cinnamon
2 tablespoons flour
2 teaspoons salt
1 cup milk
1 package (10 ounces) frozen peas

1. Pick over beans and rinse under running water. Combine beans and water in a large kettle; cover, let soak overnight. Or, to quick-soak, bring to boiling, boil 2 minutes, remove from heat; let stand 1 hour.
2. Bring soaked beans to boiling; lower heat; partially cover and simmer 35 minutes or until beans are almost tender.
3. Cut each chicken wing at joint to separate the 2 large sections. Melt butter in a large skillet; add wings and cook slowly until brown on all sides. Remove to paper toweling as they brown.
4. Add onion, carrots, curry powder and cinnamon to fat remaining in skillet. Sauté until onion is tender. Stir in flour and salt. Drain beans, reserving liquid. There should be 2 cups liquid; if not, add water to make that amount.
5. Add reserved liquid to flour mixture; cook, stirring constantly, until thickened and boiling. Add milk and peas; bring to boiling. Combine beans, chicken wings and curry sauce in a 3- to 4-quart baking dish; cover.
6. Bake in a moderate oven (350°) for 30 minutes or until beans are tender, stirring once halfway through baking.

HERBED MIXED BEAN SALAD

Makes about 6 servings.

1 can (16 ounces) red kidney beans, drained
1 can (20 ounces) white kidney beans (cannellini), drained
1 cup diced green pepper
1 cup sliced green onions
⅓ cup olive or vegetable oil
3 tablespoons wine vinegar
1 teaspoon leaf oregano, crumbled
1 teaspoon salt
¼ teaspoon pepper

1. Combine red and white kidney beans, green pepper and green onions in a medium-size bowl.
2. Combine oil, vinegar, oregano, salt and pepper in a small jar with a screw-top; cover; shake. Pour over vegetables; toss gently. Cover with plastic wrap; refrigerate 4 hours or longer to blend flavors.
3. To serve: Spoon into a shallow serving dish or bowl.

•●•

BEAN CURD See **TOFU**.

BEAN SPROUTS Used extensively in American-Chinese dishes, bean sprouts are the sprouts of small mung beans. They are available fresh and canned. Mung beans will sprout quite easily in a very few days under proper growing conditions. Fresh bean sprouts are best when cooked very quickly. See also **SPROUTS**.

Buying and Storing: Look for crisp, bright yellow to pale green sprouts, free of brown, soft, decaying spots. Store in plastic bags in the refrigerator and use within a few days or put sprouts in a bowl of water.

To Prepare: Wash in a bowlful of water; pick over to remove husks and any long thread-like roots. Drain and dry with paper toweling.

•●•

BÉARNAISE A classic French sauce resembling hollandaise but flavored with fresh herbs, shallots and vinegar. It is served over grilled meats, and is also delicious on fish, chicken and egg dishes. The sauce was originally made in a French restaurant and named in honor of King Henry IV, who was called the Great Béarnais. Béarn is a French province in the Pyrenées.

BÉARNAISE SAUCE

Makes about 1 cup.

1 tablespoon minced onion or shallot
½ teaspoon leaf tarragon, crumbled
⅛ teaspoon pepper
½ cup dry white wine
1 tablespoon tarragon vinegar
2 egg yolks
½ cup (1 stick) butter or margarine, melted
Dash cayenne
1 teaspoon chopped fresh parsley

1. Combine onion, tarragon, pepper, wine and vinegar in a small saucepan. Heat to boiling, then simmer, uncovered, 8 to 10 minutes, or until liquid measures about ⅓ cup. Strain into a cup.
2. Beat egg yolks slightly with wire whisk in the top of a double boiler; stir in about ⅓ of the melted butter. Place over *simmering* water.
3. Beat in strained liquid, alternately with remaining butter; continue beating until mixture is fluffy-thick. Remove from heat at once. Stir in cayenne and parsley.

Pictured opposite: Curried Limas and Chicken Wings, page 46

BÉCHAMEL This sauce was probably the invention of a French chef to the court of King Louis XIV. The sauce is named after Marquis Louis de Béchameil, a financier and gourmet.

Béchamel is a basic white sauce used to bind other ingredients in making soups, croquettes, or soufflés. It's made by whisking hot milk into a white roux (a blend of butter and flour). If chicken, veal or fish broth is used instead of milk, the sauce is called velouté. If the sauce is enriched with cream, it is called suprême. With grated Gruyère or Parmesan cheese added, it's called mornay sauce. See also **SAUCES**.

BÉCHAMEL SAUCE

Makes about 1 cup.

- **2 tablespoons butter**
- **2 tablespoons flour**
- **¼ teaspoon salt**
- **Dash pepper**
- **Dash ground nutmeg**
- **1 cup milk**

Heat butter in a small saucepan. Stir in the flour, salt, pepper and nutmeg. Cook until bubbly, about 1 minute. Remove from heat; stir in the milk with a wire whisk. Return to heat and cook, stirring constantly until thickened and bubbly.

•●•

BEEF The wide variety of fresh beef cuts offers almost unlimited selection for any meal and menu. Beef supplies complete protein with 8 essential amino acids. One serving of cooked ground beef (3 ounces) provides 21.8 grams of protein, or 50 per cent of the recommended daily amount, along with 225 calories, .15 milligrams of riboflavin, 4.8 milligrams niacin and 1.1 micrograms of vitamin B_{12}. Beef is also a good source of iron and zinc.

Buying Beef: All meat sold must, by law, pass an inspection for wholesomeness. Meat which is to cross state lines must be inspected by the United States Department of Agriculture (USDA). Meat sold in the state in which it is produced must pass state and city inspections.

USDA inspectors examine beef before and after slaughter to see that it comes from healthy animals and is processed under sanitary conditions. Beef which passes federal inspection is stamped with a round, purple mark made with an edible vegetable dye. The mark is stamped on wholesale cuts, so you may not see it on small, retail cuts.

Quality: The USDA has also developed a grading system which indicates the meat's quality. The top three grades are U.S. Prime, U.S. Choice, and U.S. Good. Meat marked with these grades is from young animals (usually less than two years old). Beef marked with the lower five grades (Standard, Commercial, Utility, Cutter and Canner) is from more mature, less tender animals. These grades are usually processed into sausage and canned meats, but are just as wholesome and nutritious as the meat of the higher grades.

Prime beef—the top grade—is beef which is well-marbled. Marbling refers to the small flecks of fat interspersed with the lean muscle which contributes to tenderness and flavor. Most prime beef is sold to top restaurants and meat stores.

The grades generally sold at supermarkets are Choice or Good. Choice beef contains sufficient marbling for taste and tenderness, but is less costly than prime meat. Lower-priced Good beef has less marbling (and fewer calories). It is just as tasty and nutritious, but not as tender as the higher grades.

Color: The color of fresh beef should be bright to deep red. When beef is first cut, it is dark, purplish-red. After exposure to air, the cut surface turns bright red due to a reaction with oxygen in the air. That is why ground beef is often red on the outside, while the middle is darker. The middle will also redden when it is exposed to the air.

Cost: The most accurate way to determine meat cost is to base your calculations on price per serving, rather than price per pound. Cuts which contain a large amount of bone and fat may not be as economical as higher priced cuts which contain less waste.

The chart above shows how many servings per pound you can expect from each cut of beef. Remember, do not confuse number of servings with number of people you can serve. A hearty eater can consume 3 servings at a meal!

To find the cost per serving, divide

Number of Cooked Servings (3-3½ Ounces) Per Pound from Various Beef Cuts

Roasts	
Rib Eye Roast	3
Rib Roast	2
Rump Roast	2
Rump Roast, Boneless	3
Tip Roast	3
Top Round	3
Braising Steaks	
Arm Steak	2
Blade Steak	2
Flank Steak	3
Round Steak	3
Tip Steak	3
Other Cuts	
Beef for Stew	4
Brisket	3
Ground Beef	4
Short Ribs	2
Beef Variety Meats (liver, heart, tongue, kidney)	4
Broiling Steaks	
Cubed Steak	4
Flank Steak	4
Porterhouse Steak	2
Sirloin Steak	2½
Rib Eye Steak	3
Rib Steak	2
Rib Steak, Boneless	2½
T-Bone	2
Tenderloin (Filet Mignon) Steak	3
Top Loin Steak	2
Top Loin Steak, Boneless	2½
Pot-Roasts	
Arm Pot-Roast	2
Blade Roast	2
Bottom Round Roast	3
Cross Rib Pot-Roast	2
Eye Round Roast	3
Heel of Round	2
Shoulder Pot-Roast, Boneless	2½

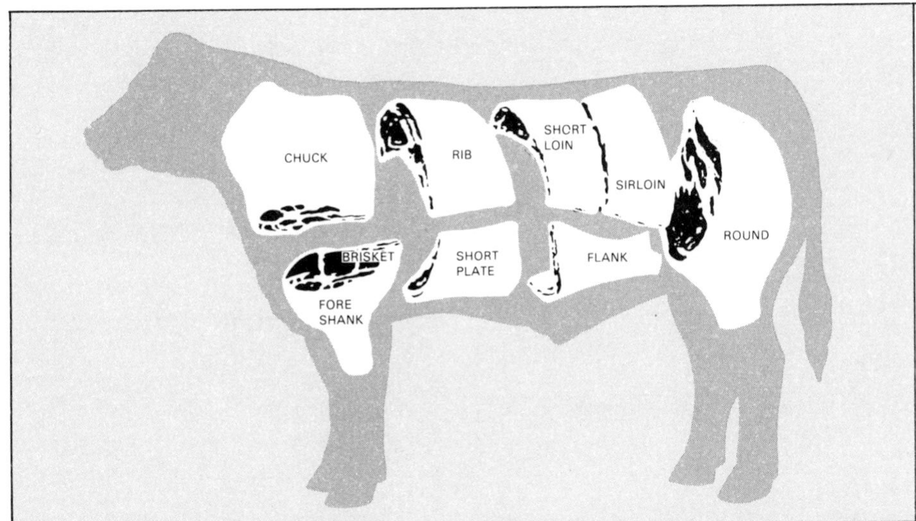

the price per pound by the number of servings per pound the cut will provide. For example, if a roast costs $1.79 a pound and that cut gives you 2½ servings a pound, your cost per serving would be 71¢.

Cut: "Which cut should I buy?" It's a tricky question with no set answers. In general, the cut to buy depends on how the meat is to be prepared. If your recipe calls for the meat to be cooked quickly or by dry heat (as in stir-frying or broiled kabobs), use a tender cut of beef. For slow, moist-heat cooking (stew, for example), a less tender cut will do.

Tender cuts come from muscles which are not used in movement and which have the least connective tissue. These muscles are found along the back of the animal and are called rib, loin or sirloin. The remaining muscles are used in movement and are less tender.

Many stores use a standardized meat-labeling system on their prepackaged meats. The label tells you the kind of meat (beef, pork, lamb, etc.), the primal or wholesale cut (chuck, rib, loin, round, etc.) which is where the cut comes from on the animal, and the retail cut (blade, arm, short rib, etc.) which tells you from what part of the primal cut the meat comes.

Since ground beef can come from several primal cuts, it is usually labeled according to the ratio of lean to fat. Again, your selection will depend on how you plan to use the meat. Ground beef or hamburger contains not less than 70% lean. Use it for burgers, chili, sloppy joes and casseroles. Lean ground beef or ground chuck has not less than 77% lean. Use it for meat loaf, meat balls and steaks. Extra lean ground beef, or ground round or sirloin, has not less than 85% lean. Use it as you would ground chuck, or when you're watching calorie and fat consumption.

Storing Beef: Fresh beef should be kept in the coldest part of the refrigerator or the compartment designed for meat storage. Prepackaged meat can be stored as purchased in the refrigerator for 2 days or in the freezer for 1 to 2 weeks. For longer freezer storage, wrap with proper freezer wrapping materials. See **FREEZING FOODS.** Beef which has been wrapped in butcher paper should be loosely rewrapped in plastic or foil and stored for up to 2 days.

Cooked beef should be wrapped or covered and stored in the refrigerator within 1 or 2 hours after cooking. Cooked beef will keep better if left in larger pieces and not cut until ready to use.

Cooking Beef

DRY HEAT METHODS FOR TENDER CUTS:

To Panbroil: For small, tender pieces cut 1-inch thick or less. Place steak or patty in heavy frying pan. Don't add fat or water and do not cover pan. Cook slowly, turning often; pour off any fat as it collects. Brown or cook to desired degree; season and serve.

To Panfry: For very thin, tender cuts or cuts made tender by pounding or cubing. They may be dusted with flour or crumbs. Heat a small amount of fat in frying pan. Add beef and brown on both sides over high heat, turning occasionally. Stir-frying is a form of panfrying used in Oriental-style cooking. A wok, large pan or electric skillet can be used. Ingre-

APPROXIMATE TIME FOR BRAISING LESS TENDER BEEF

Cut	Approximate Weight or Thickness	Approximate Total Cooking time in hours
CHUCK BLADE ROAST	3 to 5 lbs.	2 to 2½
CHUCK ARM POT ROAST	3 to 5 lbs.	2½ to 3½
CHUCK SHOULDER ROAST, BONELESS	3 to 5 lbs.	2½ to 3½
ROUND STEAK	¾ to 1 inch	1 to 1¾
CHUCK OR ROUND CUBES (1½-inch)	1½ lbs.	1½ to 2½
SHORT RIBS (2×2×4-inch pieces)	3 lbs.	1½ to 2½

APPROXIMATE TIME FOR COOKING LESS TENDER BEEF IN LIQUID

Cut	Approximate Weight	Approximate Total Cooking time in hours
FRESH OR CORNED BEEF	4 to 6 lbs.	3 to 4
SHANK CROSS CUTS	¾ to 1¼ lbs.	2 to 3

dients must be cut into uniform sizes before cooking. Sautéing is a French term for panfrying.

To Broil: For tender steaks or patties at least 1-inch thick. Place meat on broiler rack over a pan. Broil meat which is 1-inch thick 2 to 3 inches from preheated heat source. Broil thicker cuts 3 to 5 inches from heat. Turn meat with tongs rather than a fork as a fork will pierce the meat, releasing juices. A charcoal, electric or gas grill can be used for broiling.

To Roast: For large, tender roasts. Season with salt, pepper or herbs. Place beef, fat side up, on a rack in an open, shallow pan. The fat on top bastes the meat and the rack holds it out of the drippings. Insert a meat thermometer in the center of the largest muscle; do not let it touch bone or rest in fat. Do not add water or cover meat. Roast in a slow oven (300 to 325°F.). When thermometer reads 5°F. below desired degree of doneness, remove beef roast from oven and let stand 15 minutes for easier carving. See also **CARVING**. Rotisserie cooking is a form of roasting. Use large, uniformly-shaped cuts. Insert rotisserie rod lengthwise through center of roast; fasten securely. Place a drip pan under the turning beef to prevent flare-ups.

To Microwave: For tender beef roasts that are compact and uniform in shape. Boneless roasts are ideal. Place roast on a rack and cover with wax paper. Use a low power setting for a longer cooking time to get the most uniform doneness. If a roast is irregular in shape and a portion is cooking too fast, cover that piece with a bit of foil to retard cooking. To assure even cooking, turn roast or rotate the dish at intervals during the cooking time. To enhance the appearance of beef cooked by microwave, try brushing the surface with soy sauce, Worcestershire or a browning sauce. Or coat surface with bread crumbs or glaze. You can also pre-brown the roast in a frying pan or use the browning dish of the microwave. The cooking time will vary depending on the shape and size of the meat.

TEMPERATURE AND TIME FOR ROASTING BEEF

Cut	Approximate Pound Weight	Oven Temperature	Internal Meat Temperature When Done	Minutes Per Pound Roasting Time
STANDING RIB (Ribs 6 to 7 inches long)	6 to 8	300° to 325° F.	140° F. (rare)	23 to 25
			160° F. (med.)	27 to 30
			170° F. (well)	32 to 35
	4 to 6	300° to 325° F.	140° F. (rare)	26 to 32
			160° F. (med.)	34 to 38
			170° F. (well)	40 to 42
ROLLED RIB	5 to 7	300° to 325° F.	140° F. (rare)	32
			160° F. (med.)	38
			170° F. (well)	48
DELMONICO (Rib Eye)	4 to 6	350° F.	140° F. (rare)	18 to 20
			160° F. (med.)	20 to 22
			170° F. (well)	22 to 24
TENDERLOIN Whole	4 to 6	425° F.	140° F. (rare)	45 to 60*
TENDERLOIN Half	2 to 3	425° F.	140° F. (rare)	45 to 50*
ROLLED RUMP (U.S. Prime and Choice)	4 to 6	300° to 325° F.	140° to 170° F.	25 to 30
SIRLOIN TIP (U.S. Prime and Choice)	3½ to 4	300° to 325° F.	140° to 170° F.	35 to 40
	4 to 6	300° to 325° F.	140° to 170° F.	30 to 35

*Total roasting time.

APPROXIMATE TIME FOR BROILING BEEF

Cut	Approximate Weight	Approximate Thickness	Approximate Total Cooking time in Minutes RARE	MEDIUM
CHUCK BLADE STEAK (U.S. Prime and Choice)	1¼ to 1¾ lbs.	¾ in.	14	20
	1½ to 2½ lbs.	1 in.	20	25
	2 to 4 lbs.	1½ in.	35	40
RIB EYE STEAK	8 to 10 ozs.	1 in.	15	20
	12 to 14 ozs.	1½ in.	25	30
	16 to 20 ozs.	2 in.	35	45
RIB STEAK	1 to 1½ lbs.	1 in.	15	20
	1½ to 2 lbs.	1½ in.	25	30
	2 to 2½ lbs.	2 in.	35	45
PORTERHOUSE STEAK	1¼ to 2 lbs.	1 in.	20	25
	2 to 3 lbs.	1½ in.	30	35
	2½ to 3½ lbs.	2 in.	40	45
TENDERLOIN STEAK	4 to 6 ozs.	1 in.	10	15
	6 to 8 ozs.	1½ in.	15	20
TOP LOIN STEAK	1 to 1½ lbs.	1 in.	15	20
	1½ to 2 lbs.	1½ in.	25	30
	2 to 2½ lbs.	2 in.	35	45
SIRLOIN STEAK	1½ to 3 lbs.	1 in.	20	25
	2¼ to 4 lbs.	1½ in.	30	35
	3 to 5 lbs.	2 in.	40	45
TOP ROUND STEAK	1¼ to 1¾ lbs.	1 in.	20	30
	1½ to 2 lbs.	1½ in.	30	35
FLANK STEAK	1 to 1½ lbs.	—	12	14
GROUND BEEF PATTY	4 ozs.	1 in.	8	12

MOIST HEAT METHODS FOR LESS TENDER CUTS:

To Braise: Brown beef, which may be coated with flour, in its own rendered fat or in a small amount of added fat in a heavy pan. Brown on all sides slowly; add onion, herbs and about 1/4 to 1/2 cup liquid such as water, broth, vegetable juice or a marinade. Cover and cook over low heat until tender. Braising can be done on top of the range or in a slow oven (300 to 325°F.).

To Cook in Liquid: Coat beef with flour and brown on all sides in its own fat or added fat in a heavy pan. Or, omit the step above; cover beef with liquid; cover pan. Cook over low heat until beef is just tender. If you like, add vegetables and cook along with the beef until tender.

To Pressure Cook: Follow manufacturer's directions or see **PRESSURE COOKER COOKING**.

To Slow Cook: Follow manufacturer's or recipe directions.

Tenderizing Beef

Less tender cuts may be tenderized, then cooked using dry heat methods. Tenderize by pounding meat with a meat mallet, or by using a marinade or commercial tenderizing mixture.

Manually pounding cuts such as round steak with a meat mallet tenderizes by breaking down the fibers and tissue. Cube steak is round steak that a butcher has put through a special machine which tears the fiber structure and creates a flattened steak.

Marinades are usually made of an acidic liquid such as vinegar, wine, citrus or tomato juice. The acid helps soften the meat fibers and connective tissue and adds flavor. Marinades also often contain flavoring ingredients, such as garlic, pepper, etc.

Commercial tenderizing mixtures are sold in various forms and contain enzymes which break down the connective tissue. Enzymes such as papain from papaya and bromelain from pineapple are usually used in these tenderizers.

How to Pare Your Beef Bills

You can save a substantial amount of money by buying large cuts of beef and cutting and wrapping them yourself. Larger beef cuts cost less per pound since they require less handling by the butcher. All you need is a clean, sharp knife, foil or freezing paper, and tape plus a marker to identify the packages. You can divide the cut into meal-size portions such as steaks to broil or panfry; strips to stir-fry, chunks to stew and trimmings to grind. Save the bones for soup stock.

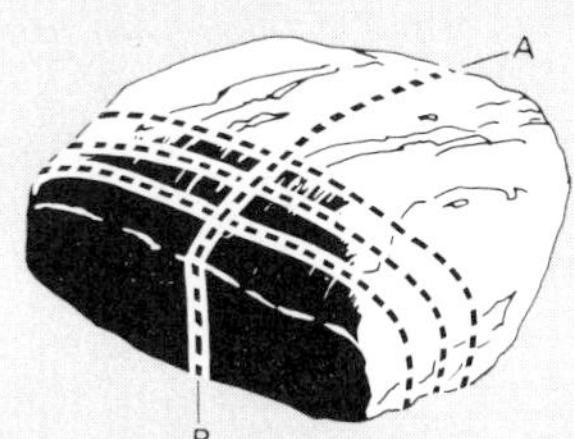

Boneless Beef Top Round

With the fat side up, use a sharp knife to first split the Top Round in half. Cut with the grain, from A to B. From either half, 2 or 3 steaks can be cut across the grain, 1 to 1½ inches thick. The remaining portions can be used as roasts. If you would like cubes for braising, cut them from the tapered end of the roasts.

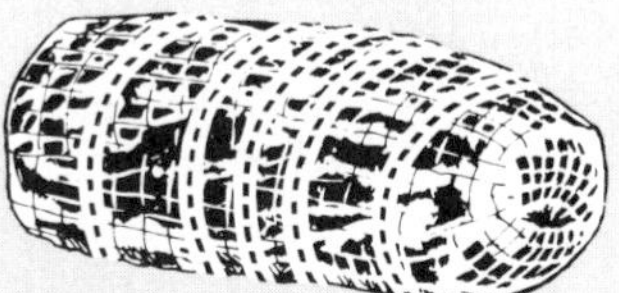

Boneless Beef Chuck Roll

If steaks for braising are a favorite, cut them with a sharp knife from the center portion. Since slicing thin steaks that hold together is difficult, for best results slice steaks about 1 inch thick. LEAVE THE NETTING OR STRINGS INTACT DURING CUTTING AND COOKING both roasts and steaks. For a roast section cut in half, tie strings to help hold shape during cooking.

Any part of the Chuck Roll is an excellent choice if you want cubes for braising or cooking in liquid or for ground beef.

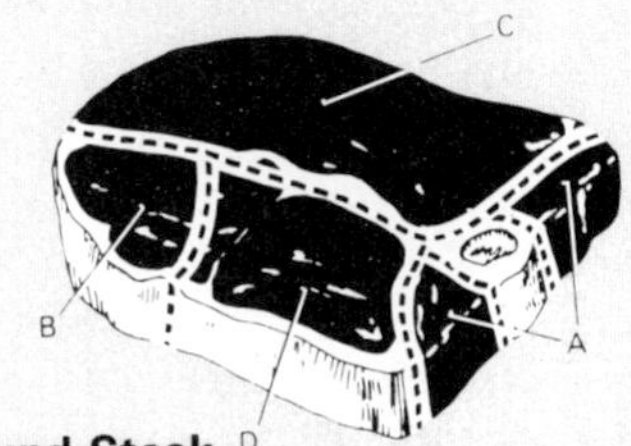

Round Steak
(1¼ to 1½ inches thick)

Cut across bone end of steak following natural seams, removing bone and small pieces of meat A attached. Remove eye section B. Cut meat from A and B into small pieces and use for stew or soup (including bone if desired), or grind.

Separate top round C from bottom round D by cutting along natural seams. The larger top round is the most tender part of the round steak. Score if desired, marinate and broil to rare or medium. Carve in thin slices across the grain.

The bottom round D can be chilled and cut into thin strips for braising or marinating and stir-frying. Or it can be sliced into two thin steaks, pounded and braised as for Swiss steak.

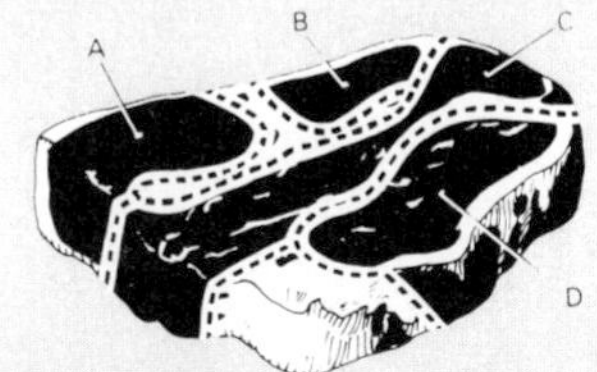

7-Bone Pot-Roast
(2 to 2¼ inches thick)

Cut around blade bone and remove sections A and B. Section A is the top blade and the most tender part of this cut. Remove membrane separating section A into two pieces; cut each into slices one-half inch thick. Panfry to rare or medium.

Divide remaining meat by cutting along natural seam between sections C and D. Remove bone from D. Cut meat from D and B into cubes; cook in liquid for stew or soup or grind.

Braise section C as pot-roast. Or chill and cut into thin strips to stir-fry or into four thin steaks to marinate and broil.

BEEF AND VEGETABLE KABOBS

Grill 12 to 15 minutes.
Makes 4 servings.

- **1 chuck steak, 1½ inches thick (about 2 pounds)**
- **½ pint cherry tomatoes**
- **½ pound mushrooms**
- **2 green peppers**
- **1 jar (16 ounces) whole onions in liquid**
- **1 jar (6 ounces) marinated artichoke hearts**
- **½ cup vegetable oil**
- **¼ cup honey**
- **2 tablespoons vinegar**
- **2 tablespoons soy sauce**
- **1 large clove garlic, minced**
- **2 tablespoons minced parsley**
- **1 teaspoon ground ginger**
- **1 teaspoon coarse salt**
- **½ teaspoon cracked pepper**

1. Cut steak into 1½-inch cubes. Prepare vegetables, leaving tomatoes and mushroom caps whole if small; seed peppers and cut into squares; drain onions and artichoke hearts, reserving liquids.
2. Combine oil, honey, vinegar, soy sauce, garlic, parsley, ginger, salt and pepper with reserved liquids. Pour marinade mixture into a large, shallow nonmetal dish. Add meat cubes.
3. Cover dish and refrigerate. Let marinate for 1 to 24 hours, turning occasionally.
4. Thread vegetables, except peppers, on skewers and brush generously with marinade. Remove meat from marinade. Pat with paper toweling to remove excess marinade. Thread meat and peppers alternately on other skewers.
5. Grill meat 5 inches from hot coals 12 to 15 minutes for rare, turning skewers several times and basting with the marinade. Grill vegetables about 5 to 8 minutes, brushing with marinade and turning several times until tender.

ROAST RIBS OF BEEF

Makes 12 servings.

Rub surface of a *3-rib (seven-inch cut) standing rib roast* with *1 teaspoon salt* and *¼ teaspoon pepper.* Place, fat side up, in shallow roasting pan. Do not cover; do not add water. No rack is necessary. Insert meat thermometer into thickest part of roast, with bulb not touching bone or resting in fat. Roast in a slow oven (325°) 20 minutes per pound for rare (140°), 22 to 25 minutes for medium (160°) and 27 to 30 minutes for well-done (170°). Let meat rest in a warm place 30 minutes before carving.

BROILED STEAKS PERSILLADE

The persillade is the Provençal seasoning of chopped garlic and parsley. It should always be nicely browned and crisped in butter or olive oil before being used as a seasoning for meats or vegetables.

Makes 6 servings.

- **6 individual beef steaks, cut ¾-inch thick (top loin, club or rib)**
- **¼ cup vegetable oil**
- **1 teaspoon salt**
- **½ teaspoon pepper**
- **2 large green peppers, seeded and cut into ¼-inch strips**
- **2 large red peppers, seeded and cut in ¼-inch strips**
- **2 tablespoons butter or margarine**
- **2 large cloves garlic, minced**
- **½ cup chopped fresh parsley**

1. Trim the steaks of fat and gristle. Rub the steaks on both sides with 1 tablespoon of the oil. Put them on a rack over a broiler pan.
2. Broil steaks 3 to 4 inches from heat 3 minutes on the first side; sprinkle with half the salt and pepper; turn. Broil on second side 4 more minutes; sprinkle with remaining salt and pepper. Remove to a hot platter.
3. While steaks broil, heat 2 tablespoons of the oil in a skillet. Sauté the peppers, stirring often, until they are heated through, about 5 minutes. Remove to platter with steaks.
4. Heat the last tablespoon of oil and butter in the skillet. Sauté garlic and parsley; spoon persillade over steaks.

SPICY "SLOPPY JOES"

Beef, barbecue sauce and pinto beans team up for this South-of-the-Border quickie.

Makes 6 servings.

- **1 pound ground chuck**
- **1 can (1 pound) pinto beans in sugar and spice sauce**
- **½ cup bottled barbecue or hot barbecue sauce**
- **½ cup frozen cut sweet red and green peppers**

1. Brown beef in a large skillet; pour off fat.
2. Add beans, barbecue sauce and peppers. Cook, stirring frequently, until bubbly-hot. Serve over warmed hamburger buns, if you wish.

ROAST BEEF

Serve with baked yams and broccoli.

Roast at 325° for 1 hour and 10 minutes.
Makes 12 servings.

- **1 boneless beef rump roast (3½ pounds)**
- **1 teaspoon salt**
- **¼ teaspoon pepper**
- **Beef Pan Gravy *(recipe follows)***

1. Rub roast with salt and pepper; place, fat side up, on rack in roasting pan. Do not add water or cover pan. If using a meat thermometer, insert bulb into center of meat.
2. Roast in a slow oven (325°), allowing 20 minutes per pound or about 1 hour and 10 minutes for rare meat (140°); 30 minutes per pound or about 1 hour and 45 minutes for medium (160°).
3. Place roast on cutting board; allow to stand for 15 minutes for easier carving.
4. Cut roast into thin slices. Serve with Beef Pan Gravy.

Beef Pan Gravy: Skim off all fat from roasting pan into a cup, leaving juices in pan. Return 1 tablespoon fat to pan; blend in 1 tablespoon flour. Cook, stirring, just until mixture bubbles. Stir in 1 cup water slowly; continue cooking and stirring, scraping baked-on juices from bottom of pan, until gravy thickens and bubbles 3 minutes. Taste; season with salt and pepper if needed. Makes 1 cup.

Pictured opposite: Roast Beef, page 52

MARINATED FILET OF BEEF

Other cuts can also be used in this recipe.

Roast at 425° for 45 minutes.
Makes 12 servings.

- **1 filet of beef (about 4 pounds) OR: 1 rolled boned rib roast of beef, or eye-round roast, or sirloin tip roast (about 4 pounds)**
- **1 cup soy sauce**
- **½ cup medium or dry sherry**
- **⅓ cup olive oil**
- **3 cloves garlic, minced**
- **2 teaspoons ground ginger**

1. Trim filet if needed. In a large bowl (not aluminum), mix soy sauce, sherry, olive oil, garlic and ginger. Place roast in mixture in bowl. Refrigerate 4 hours or overnight, turning roast several times, to season.
2. Remove roast from refrigerator 1 hour before cooking and let stand at room temperature.
3. Place roast on a rack in a roasting pan. Insert meat thermometer into center of thickest part.
4. Roast in a hot oven (425°), brushing with soy mixture 3 or 4 times, 45 to 50 minutes, or until thermometer registers 140° for rare. For medium rare, continue roasting to 150°. Do not overcook.
5. Remove roast to a deep platter; pour pan juices over top. Slice and serve.

STEAK AU POIVRE

Makes 6 to 8 servings.

- **1 sirloin steak (about 3 pounds)**
- **Salt**
- **Coarsely ground black pepper**
- **2 tablespoons olive oil or clarified butter**
- **¼ cup brandy or rum**

1. Rub steak on both sides with salt and pepper.
2. Heat oil or butter in a large skillet. Pan-fry steak over high heat to desired doneness.
3. Remove steak from pan to heated platter. Add brandy or rum to pan. Mix juices; pour over steak. Serve immediately.

OVEN-BARBECUED BRISKET OF BEEF

One of the simplest and easiest ways to cook beef for flavor and tender eating.

Bake at 350° for 3 hours.
Makes 8 servings.

- **1 lean brisket of beef (4 to 5 pounds)**
- **Liquid smoke (optional)**
- **½ recipe Texas Barbecue Sauce (2 cups) *(recipe follows)***

1. Center a 24-inch length of 18-inch heavy-duty foil in a 13×9×2-inch baking pan.
2. Place brisket on center of foil. Add liquid smoke to sauce if you wish; pour sauce over meat. Bring ends of foil together evenly; fold over and continue folding down to top of meat. Fold sides up to make a neat sealed package.
3. Bake package in the pan in a moderate oven (350°) for 3 hours or until meat is tender.
4. Remove from oven. Carefully open foil; lift meat to heated serving platter. Pour sauce from foil into sauce dish. Skim off excess fat. Serve sauce with meat.

TEXAS BARBECUE SAUCE

Here's a real winner you'll want to make again and again. Stored in clean jars in the refrigerator, it will keep for months.

Makes about 4½ cups.

- **2 medium-size onions, finely chopped (1 cup)**
- **1 clove garlic, finely chopped**
- **¼ cup vegetable oil**
- **2 tablespoons chili powder**
- **2 cups catsup**
- **1 cup cider or white vinegar**
- **½ cup lemon juice**
- **¼ cup Worcestershire sauce**
- **⅓ cup firmly packed brown sugar**
- **2 tablespoons prepared mustard**
- **1 tablespoon celery seeds**
- **2 teaspoons cumin seeds, crushed**
- **2 tablespoons butter or margarine**

1. Sauté onions and garlic in oil in a large saucepan until golden and tender, 10 minutes; stir in chili powder and cook 1 minute.
2. Add all remaining ingredients except butter; bring to boiling. Lower heat; simmer uncovered, stirring often, for 30 minutes. Stir in butter.

HEARTY BEEF STEW

A savory stew with an abundance of spring vegetables.

Makes 8 servings.

- **3 tablespoons olive or vegetable oil**
- **3 pounds lean chuck or round, cut into 1½- to 2-inch cubes**
- **3 tablespoons finely chopped shallots**
- **1 clove garlic, minced**
- **3 tablespoons flour**
- **1 can condensed beef broth**
- **1 can (16 ounces) tomatoes OR: 1 cup peeled and chopped fresh tomatoes**
- **1½ teaspoons salt**
- **½ teaspoon leaf thyme, crumbled**
- **12 small white onions, peeled**
- **4 small turnips, pared and quartered**
- **3 to 4 carrots, pared and cut into 2-inch lengths**
- **12 small new potatoes, peeled (1 pound)**
- **1 package (10 ounces) frozen peas**
- **2 tablespoons chopped parsley**

1. Heat oil in a large kettle or Dutch oven; brown beef, a few pieces at a time. Remove pieces as they brown to a bowl.
2. Remove all but 1 tablespoon fat from kettle; add shallots and garlic; sauté, stirring often, 2 minutes, or until golden-brown. Sprinkle flour over shallots; cook over moderate heat, stirring.
3. Stir in beef broth and tomatoes; bring to boiling, stirring constantly to loosen browned bits. Return beef to kettle. Stir in salt and thyme. Bring to boiling; lower heat, cover. Simmer 1 hour. Skim off fat, if any.
4. Add onions, turnips, carrots and potatoes to beef, pushing them down under liquid; cover; simmer 45 minutes longer, or until beef and vegetables are tender. Stir in peas; cover; simmer 5 to 10 minutes longer. Sprinkle with parsley. Taste, and add more salt, if necessary.

Pictured opposite: Hearty Beef Stew, page 54

FLANK STEAK WITH DILL

Makes 6 servings.

1½ pounds trimmed flank steak or skirt steak
¼ cup (½ stick) butter or margarine
1½ cups frozen chopped onions
1 large clove garlic, minced
1 tablespoon flour
1 teaspoon salt
¼ teaspoon pepper
1 container (8 ounces) whole milk yogurt
¼ cup chopped fresh dill
Hot cooked rice

1. Cut flank steak in half lengthwise and slice each half into 1/16-inch thick slices against the grain.
2. Melt 2 tablespoons of the butter in a large skillet. Add ½ of the meat and cook just until meat loses its red color. Remove with slotted spoon to bowl. Add remaining meat to juices in skillet and cook just until meat loses its red color. Remove with spoon to bowl.
3. Add remaining 2 tablespoons butter to skillet with onions and garlic. Cook over high heat until liquid evaporates from onions, about 1 minute, stirring occasionally.
4. Return meat to skillet. Sprinkle with flour, salt and pepper. Add yogurt and dill, stirring thoroughly. Cover; simmer 10 minutes or until tender. Serve over rice. Garnish with dill, if you wish.

SPICY SZECHUAN SHREDDED BEEF AND VEGETABLES

Makes 6 servings.

2 tablespoons finely minced fresh ginger root
OR: 1 teaspoon ground ginger
1 clove garlic, crushed
¼ teaspoon ground cloves
¼ teaspoon ground cinnamon
⅛ teaspoon fennel seeds, crushed
⅛ teaspoon anise seeds, crushed
⅛ to ¼ teaspoon crushed red pepper
3 tablespoons soy sauce
3 tablespoons dry sherry
1 tablespoon vegetable oil
1 pound boneless top round
3 tablespoons vegetable oil
3 medium-size carrots, finely shredded
3 medium-size celery stalks, thinly sliced
8 green onions, thinly sliced
Hot cooked rice

1. Combine ginger, garlic, cloves, cinnamon, fennel, anise, crushed pepper, soy, sherry and the 1 tablespoon oil in a jar with a screw-top lid. Shake marinade well to mix.
2. Cut the beef in very thin strips about the size and shape of shoestring potatoes with a sharp knife. (It will make slicing easier if you put the beef in the freezer for an hour.) Put beef strips in large bowl. Shake marinade again and pour over beef; toss; let stand at room temperature for 1 hour, turning once or twice.
3. Heat 2 tablespoons of the remaining oil in a wok or large skillet until a shred of carrot will sizzle, then add the carrots, celery and green onions. Stir-fry about 3 minutes or just until crisp-tender.
4. Quickly add the remaining tablespoon of oil, the beef and any remaining marinade. Stir-fry 3 minutes longer or until beef is no longer bright red. Serve with hot cooked rice.

DEVILED BEEF TURNOVERS

Ground beef holds a spirited onion stuffing.

Makes 4 servings.

1 large onion, halved and thinly sliced
¼ cup (½ stick) butter or margarine
1 can (12 ounces) beer
1½ teaspoons salt
1½ pounds ground chuck or round
1 tablespoon vegetable oil
1 tablespoon flour
1 tablespoon brown sugar
2 tablespoons bottled steak sauce
1 tablespoon prepared mustard

1. Combine onion, butter, ½ cup of the beer and ½ teaspoon of the salt in a large skillet. Heat to boiling, stirring frequently. Cook until beer has evaporated and onions are golden. Remove with slotted spoon to bowl, leaving drippings in pan; cool.
2. Divide chuck into 4 balls; roll out each between wax paper to a 6-inch circle. Dust lightly with flour if meat sticks to paper.
3. Place a quarter of the sautéed onions in the center of each circle; fold patty in half, enclosing the filling. Crimp edges firmly to seal.
4. Add oil to drippings in skillet; heat over medium heat. Pan-fry turnovers 4 minutes on each side or until done as you like them. Place on serving platter; keep warm.
5. Stir flour into pan drippings in skillet. Stir in remaining 1 cup of the beer until sauce thickens and boils 1 minute. Stir in remaining 1 teaspoon salt, brown sugar, steak sauce and mustard until well blended. Spoon sauce over turnovers. Garnish platter with watercress, if you wish.

BEEF SUKIYAKI

Makes 4 servings.

1 pound boneless sirloin steak, cut 2 inches thick
3 celery stalks, cut into ½-inch lengths
¼ pound mushrooms, sliced
6 green onions, cut into 1-inch pieces
1 can (8 ounces) water chestnuts, drained and sliced
¼ pound fresh spinach, washed and torn into pieces
2 tablespoons vegetable oil
½ cup canned beef broth
¼ cup soy sauce
¼ cup dry sherry
1 tablespoon sugar

1. Slice beef diagonally across the grain into uniformly thin strips. Arrange meat and vegetables on large plate.
2. Heat oil in a large skillet; brown meat quickly. Push meat to one side and add vegetables except spinach, keeping each type in a separate area of the pan. Stir gently to cook.
3. Combine broth, soy sauce, sherry and sugar in a small bowl. When vegetables are tender but still crisp, pour in soy mixture. Cook 5 more minutes.
4. Add spinach and cook until wilted, about 3 minutes. Stir and serve.

ITALIAN BEEF ROLLS

Say good-bye to long cooking when you make this quickie.

Makes 4 servings.

- **4 minute round steaks, or beef for braciole, or cube steaks (1 pound)**
- **1 teaspoon meat tenderizer with steak sauce flavor**
- **1 teaspoon leaf oregano, crumbled**
- **¼ pound sliced Genoa salami**
- **½ an 8-ounce package mozzarella, cut into 4 slices**
- **¼ cup (½ stick) butter or margarine**
- **1 cup water**
- **1 bar (1⁵⁄₁₆ ounces) mushroom concentrate for gravy**
- **2 tablespoons dry red wine**

1. Pound meat with a mallet or rolling pin until evenly thinned, ⅛-inch thick, but do not pound through. Sprinkle with meat tenderizer and oregano.
2. Overlap salami slices and 1 slice cheese, cut to fit, on each steak piece. Roll up jelly-roll fashion, tucking ends in to enclose filling; fasten with wooden picks.
3. Melt butter in large skillet. Sauté steak rolls, turning to brown on all sides, until meat is done, about 5 minutes. Remove meat to serving platter; take out the wooden picks.
4. Add water to pan drippings; crumble in mushroom concentrate for gravy; add wine; cook until gravy thickens. Spoon some gravy over rolls. Pour remainder in gravy boat and pass at table. Sprinkle with chopped parsley, if you wish.

CHICKEN-FRIED STEAK WITH PAN GRAVY

Sometimes called "country-fried" but always called good eating.

Makes 6 servings.

- **1¾ pounds round steak, sliced ½-inch thick**
  OR: **6 cube steaks (about 1¾ pounds)**
- **2 eggs**
- **2 tablespoons water**
- **⅓ cup all-purpose flour**
- **⅓ cup cornmeal**
- **1 teaspoon salt**
- **½ teaspoon pepper**
- **Flour**
- **4 to 6 tablespoons vegetable oil**

Pan Gravy:

- **2 tablespoons flour**
- **1½ cups milk (about)**
- **½ teaspoon salt**
- **⅛ teaspoon pepper**

1. Pound steak to ¼-inch thick, or ask butcher to tenderize; cut into 6 pieces.
2. Beat eggs and water together in pie plate. Mix flour, cornmeal, salt and pepper on wax paper. Dip steaks first in plain flour, then in egg mixture. Dip in seasoned flour mixture to coat well.
3. Brown meat, 3 pieces at a time, in hot oil on both sides in a large heavy skillet. Return all meat to skillet; lower heat; cover. Cook 20 minutes or until tender. Remove steaks to heated platter.
4. To prepare Pan Gravy, pour off all but 3 tablespoons of the pan drippings; blend in flour. Stir in milk, salt and pepper. Continue cooking and stirring until gravy thickens and bubbles 1 minute. If gravy is too thick add more milk.

BEEF AND BEANS

This hearty meal-in-a-dish is the modern version of one that sustained many a cattle driver along the old Chisholm Trail.

Bake at 325° for 1½ hours.
Makes 8 servings.

- **½ pound small dried lima beans**
- **½ pound dried pinto or kidney beans**
- **6 cups water**
- **3 bacon slices**
- **4 cross cuts beef shank (3½ to 4 pounds)**
- **2 tablespoons flour**
- **2 large onions, chopped (2 cups)**
- **1 can (35 ounces) plum tomatoes, undrained**
- **3 teaspoons salt**
- **½ teaspoon pepper**
- **¼ teaspoon crushed red pepper**
- **1 teaspoon leaf thyme, crumbled**
- **1 bay leaf**

1. Pick over beans and rinse; place in a large saucepan or kettle and add water. Let stand overnight to soak.
2. Next day, bring beans and liquid slowly to boiling; cover. Simmer 30 minutes. Drain beans, reserving liquid to use later.
3. Meanwhile, sauté bacon until crisp in a large skillet. Remove bacon and set aside. Coat beef shanks with flour. Brown on all sides in bacon drippings; transfer as they brown to a 12-cup baking dish. Add beans to baking dish.
4. Add onions to skillet; sauté, stirring often, until lightly browned and tender, 10 minutes. Stir in tomatoes, salt, pepper, red pepper, thyme and bay leaf; bring to boiling, stirring and crushing tomatoes. Pour over beans and beef shanks. Cover.
5. Bake in a slow oven (325°) for 1½ to 2 hours or until tender, stirring once or twice and adding some reserved bean liquid if mixture becomes dry. Crumble bacon over top of beans before serving.

OLÉ CHILI PIE

Bake at 375° for 18 minutes.
Makes 4 to 6 servings.

- **1 package (8½ ounces) corn muffin mix**
- **1 pound ground beef**
- **1 package (1⅛ ounces) taco seasoning mix**
- **3 ounces natural Colby or Cheddar cheese, shredded (¾ cup)**
- **1 cup shredded lettuce**
- **1 small tomato, seeded and chopped**
- **¼ cup sliced pitted ripe olives**

1. Preheat oven to 375°. Prepare corn muffin mix following label directions. Spread batter evenly in bottom of a greased 9-inch pie plate.
2. Bake in a preheated moderate oven (375°) for 18 minutes or until golden brown.
3. Meanwhile, prepare ground beef with taco seasoning mix, following label directions; spoon over hot cornbread. Sprinkle with about half the cheese. Arrange lettuce, tomato, remaining cheese and the olives on top of pie.

BEER Any fermented malt beverage — ale, lager, malt liquor, stout, porter. In the United States, lager is the most popular type.

Although most beer is made from barley, it can be — and has been — brewed from many grains including wheat, oats, rice, millet, corn and sorghum. Egyptians at least 5,000 years ago are credited with making a brew from grain.

To produce beer, barley is soaked in water and allowed to germinate under precise conditions. This process, called malting, transforms the starch in the grain into a sugar called maltose. The germinated barley is called malt. The malt is dried and milled, then mixed with water and cooked.

After the grain is cooked to the desired degree, the liquid, called malt extract or wort, is separated from the mash and drained into the brew kettle. The extract is boiled with hops — the dried flowers of the hop vine — which add a bitter flavor. Afterwards, the extract is strained, cooled and placed in fermenting containers. At this stage the yeast is added and fermentation begins to take place. During fermentation, the yeast converts the sugars into alcohol and carbon dioxide.

The flavor of each beer varies according to the ingredients used: the grain(s) used, the amount of hops added, type of water and yeast used. Barley, when properly malted, is expensive and gives a strong, malt-flavored brew. Often, cheaper grains such as rice, corn or wheat are mixed with barley. They are called adjuncts. Beer made with adjuncts is lighter in character and taste. Many of the American beermakers pride themselves in the use of adjuncts to achieve the individual characteristics of their brew.

Each brewery uses its own strain of yeast, which also flavors the brew. Two types of yeast are used: One, called top-fermenting yeast, is used to make ale, porter and stout. The other type, bottom-fermenting yeast, is used in lager beer.

Types of Beer

Ale has an alcohol content of 5% or more by weight and a strong hop flavor. Dark ales are also rich in malt flavor.

Bock is a strong, sweet, dark beer. Traditionally, it was brewed in the winter for spring consumption, but it is now available year-round.

Lager is a German word meaning "to store" — that is, the beer is stored or aged. Most are aged only a few weeks, some only a few days. Lagers may be light or dark in color. The alcohol content usually ranges from about 4% to 5%.

Light or *Lite* now refers to lowered alcohol content in beer rather than color or flavor. Light beers contain about one-third fewer calories than the average beer. Most light beers are lagers with about 3.2% alcohol.

Malt liquor is a lager beer with a higher alcohol content — up to 7%.

Pilsener originated in Pilsen, Czechoslovakia. It is a lager beer that is light in appearance, but full-bodied and bitter.

Porter is a very dark ale similar to *stout* but not as high in alcohol or strong in hop flavor. It has a strong malt taste and may be sweet or dry.

Cooking with Beer: Beer adds its subtle flavor to the recipes of many countries. It can be used in a marinade, as a seafood poaching liquid, or in making light batters for frying foods. Once it is cooked, all trace of alcohol disappears.

WELSH RAREBIT

The cheese mixture can be prepared ahead and refrigerated for 1 to 2 days. Reheat in double boiler.

Makes 4 servings.

- **8 ounces shredded sharp Cheddar cheese (2 cups)**
- **1 tablespoon flour**
- **½ teaspoon dry mustard**
- **1 tablespoon butter or margarine**
- **⅛ to ¼ teaspoon liquid hot pepper seasoning**
- **¼ cup beer or ale**
- **8 slices white bread**

1. Combine cheese, flour, mustard, butter and pepper seasoning in a medium-size saucepan. Stir in beer. Cook over low heat, stirring constantly, until cheese is melted.
2. Trim crusts from bread. Cut bread into triangles. Toast bread on one side only.
3. Pour the melted cheese over the toasted side; serve immediately.

BATTER-FRIED ONION RINGS

Here's a popular American side dish that's made better with beer batter. You might also like to try the batter on other favorite foods such as shrimp, fish, chicken, or other vegetables.

Makes 6 servings.

- **1½ cups all-purpose flour**
- **1 can (12 ounces) beer, active or flat, cold or at room temperature**
- **3 very large yellow onions or Bermuda onions**
- **1 quart vegetable oil**

1. Combine flour and beer in a large bowl and blend thoroughly, using a rotary beater. Cover; allow batter to stand at room temperature for at least 3 hours. (If batter is too thick, stir in some water.)
2. Twenty minutes before the batter is ready, preheat oven to 200°. Place layers of paper toweling on a jelly-roll pan. Carefully peel the papery skins from the onions so that you do not cut into the outside onion layer. Cut onions into ¼-inch thick slices. Separate the slices into rings.
3. Pour enough oil in deep fryer or kettle to come 2 inches up the side of the pan. Heat to 375° on a deep-fat frying thermometer.
4. Dip a few onion rings into the batter with metal tongs, then carefully place them in the hot fat. Fry rings, turning them once or twice until they are an even, delicate golden color. Transfer to the paper-lined jelly roll pan. To keep warm, place them on the middle shelf of the preheated oven until all the onion rings have been fried.

Pictured opposite: Spicy Szechuan Shredded Beef and Vegetables, page 56

BEER-BRAISED SAUSAGES

Makes 6 servings.

2 pounds pork sausages
4 medium-size onions, thinly sliced
1 can or bottle (12 ounces) beer or ale
½ teaspoon leaf thyme, crumbled
½ teaspoon salt
¼ teaspoon pepper

1. Prick sausages all over with fork. Cook in a large skillet, turning occasionally, until brown. Remove sausages to paper toweling to drain.
2. Pour off all but 3 tablespoons fat. Add onions to skillet; sauté until soft, about 10 minutes.
3. Add beer, thyme, salt and pepper. Heat to boiling; lower heat; simmer, covered, 10 minutes.
4. Return sausages to skillet. Cover and simmer 25 minutes. Serve with mashed potatoes, if you wish.

BELGIAN BEEF STEW

Makes 6 servings.

¼ pound lean bacon, diced
20 small white onions, peeled
1 large clove garlic, minced
2 pounds boneless chuck or round, cut into 1½-inch cubes
2 tablespoons flour
2 teaspoons salt
¼ teaspoon pepper
1 can or bottle (12 ounces) dark beer
1 tablespoon lemon juice

1. Pour boiling water over bacon in a large skillet and let stand 1 minute. Drain. Cook bacon until limp and transparent. Add onions and garlic. Cook, stirring frequently, until they are golden.
2. Transfer bacon and onions to a Dutch oven or flameproof casserole. Add beef cubes, a few pieces at a time, to the fat in the skillet and brown over high heat. As the cubes brown, transfer to casserole.
3. Add flour, salt, pepper and beer to casserole. Bring to boiling. Lower heat. Cover and simmer 1½ hours or until meat is tender. Check for moisture and, if necessary, add a little more beer.
4. Taste for seasoning and add more salt and pepper. Remove from heat. Stir in lemon juice. Serve with noodles, if you wish.

BEET It's been cultivated for centuries, not only for the fleshy root, but for the tasty leaves, as well. Red beets grew wild along the coast of western Europe and North Africa. Germans were first to cultivate them. Yellow or golden beets, once favored over red beets, are now found only in home gardens. Other varieties are grown for animal feed; still others for sugar production.

Beets are delicious for salads, as a relish, vegetable or soup. A serving of two 2-inch beets (100 grams) has 30 calories. Though the roots are not high in vitamins, the green leaves have lots of vitamin A and calcium.

Buying and Storing Summer is the peak season for fresh beets though they can be found in some markets year round. They are sold in bunches with or without the leaves. Look for medium to small size roots that are firm and unblemished. Beet greens are best when the roots are very small. Look for unwilted leaves. Store fresh beets or leaves in the refrigerator in plastic bags.

Beets are also sold canned, packed in water. The roots are either left whole, sliced, diced or cut into julienne pieces. They are also available pickled.

To Prepare: Cut off the greens about 2 inches from the top of the roots; discard greens if they are large or tough. Scrub roots with a brush. If using leaves, wash well. Cut off all the lower stems of the leaves.

To Cook: Place the roots in a saucepan; cover them with water. Boil covered until a skewer can be inserted easily through the root, from 15 to 45 minutes. If using leaves, add and cook just until tender. Pour off water. With slotted spoon, remove beets and slip off skins. Return to pan. Add butter or margarine or bacon drippings, salt and a bit of lemon juice or vinegar. Reheat and serve.

To Microwave: Place ½ cup water and ½ teaspoon salt in a casserole dish. Add 1 bunch beets (about 5 medium); pierce skin with fork. Cover. Microwave on high power 11 minutes. Stir. Microwave 5 to 10 minutes more or until tender.

BEET SALAD

Makes 4 servings.

1 jar (16 ounces) pickled beets, drained
OR: 1 can (16 ounces) sliced beets, drained
Lemon Vinaigrette Dressing *(recipe follows)*
1 navel orange
1 small onion, chopped (¼ cup)
Lettuce
3 tablespoons chopped parsley

1. Arrange beets in a shallow dish; drizzle with half of the Lemon Vinaigrette Dressing.
2. Use a sharp knife to peel orange. Cut into thin slices; cut slices in half.
3. Arrange orange slices over beets; spread onion over orange. Pour remaining dressing over all. Cover; refrigerate 30 minutes.
4. Place small lettuce leaf on each of 4 chilled salad plates. Arrange beet salad over lettuce. Spoon a little dressing over each serving; sprinkle with parsley.

LEMON VINAIGRETTE DRESSING

Makes about ¼ cup.

3 tablespoons olive or vegetable oil
1 tablespoon lemon juice
¼ teaspoon salt
⅛ teaspoon pepper
⅛ teaspoon dry mustard
1 teaspoon finely chopped parsley

Measure all ingredients into a small bowl. Use a wire whisk to blend thoroughly.

SWEET-SOUR GLAZED BEETS

Just the right amount of vinegar makes this sauce so good with beets.

Makes 4 servings.

2 bunches beets
¼ cup sugar
1 tablespoon cornstarch
¼ teaspoon salt
½ cup cider vinegar

1. Wash beets. Cut off all but 2 inches of tops; leave root end intact.
2. Place beets in saucepan; add water to cover. Bring water to boiling. Cook beets, covered, 35 to 45 minutes (depending on size), or until tender. Drain.
3. Allow beets to cool slightly; trim root and stem ends; slip skins off. Slice beets. (You should get 2 cups.)
4. Combine sugar, cornstarch and salt in a saucepan; add vinegar. Cook over medium heat, stirring constantly until thickened and bubbly.
5. Add beets to sauce; heat 3 minutes, stirring gently.

PICKLED BEETS

You can eat these beets ten days after you make them, or you can "put them up" and eat them all winter.

Makes 1 quart or 4 half-pints.

8 small beets (2 pounds)
1 cup cider vinegar
1 teaspoon salt
¼ cup sugar
5 peppercorns
1 teaspoon pickling spices
1 bay leaf
Fresh dill (optional)

1. Wash and rinse a 1-quart canning jar and lid, or, if "putting up," 4 half-pint jars and lids. Keep jars in simmering water.
2. Scrub beets; trim, leaving 1 inch of the tops and the root ends attached. Cook, covered, in boiling salted water to cover, 40 minutes or until barely tender. Beets should be somewhat firm. Drain, reserving 1 cup of the cooking liquid. Rinse beets in cold running water; slip off skins, roots and tops; slice.
3. Fill the jar or jars with beet slices. Combine the reserved cup of cooking liquid with vinegar, salt, sugar, peppercorns, pickling spices and bay leaf. Bring to boiling; pour into filled jars to ¼-inch from tops.
4. Seal jar and refrigerate for 10 days before serving.
5. For canning, seal the half-pint jars. Process for 10 minutes in boiling water bath. Cool; check seals. Label and store in a cool, dry place.

•●•

BELGIAN ENDIVE See **ENDIVE** and **CHICORY.**

BENNE Known also as sesame seeds. The word Benne (pronounced like Benny) is of African origin. The seeds grow in the low lands of South Carolina and are used for cookies, candies and crackers. See also **SESAME SEEDS.**

BENNE STICKS

Bake at 325° for 30 minutes.
Makes 16 sticks.

⅓ cup sesame seeds
1 cup *sifted* all-purpose flour
⅛ teaspoon salt
Dash cayenne
3 tablespoons butter or margarine
3 tablespoons shortening
Ice water

1. Spread the sesame seeds on a shallow baking pan.
2. Bake in a slow oven (325°) for 15 minutes or until golden, stirring twice. Cool seeds.
3. Combine the flour, salt and cayenne in a bowl. With a pastry blender or the fingertips, work the butter and shortening in until the mixture resembles coarse crumbs.
4. Add the cooled sesame seeds. While stirring with a fork, add 2 to 3 tablespoons ice water or enough to make a dough. Gather into a ball.
5. Roll out the dough on a lightly-floured board into a rectangle ⅛-inch thick. Cut into sticks 4 inches by ½ inch. Transfer sticks to a cookie sheet.
6. Bake sticks in a preheated slow oven (325°) for 15 minutes or until golden. Cool on a wire rack. Store in a tightly covered container.

•●•

BERRIES Small, fleshy fruit. There are dozens of varieties. For specific information, see **BLACKBERRIES, BLUEBERRIES, CRANBERRIES, CURRANTS, GOOSEBERRIES, RASPBERRIES, STRAWBERRIES.**

Buying and Storing: Berries are highly perishable and bruise easily. Refrigerate and use in 1 to 2 days. Or freeze on cookie sheets and when firm, pack into containers. They will keep 2 months in a refrigerator-freezer or up to a year in a deep freezer at 0°F. or below.

•●•

BEVERAGE Any hot or cold drink. Following is a collection of beverages for all occasions. See also **APERITIF, COCKTAIL, COFFEE, LIQUEUR, PUNCH, TEA, WATER, WINE.**

PINK TOMATO DRINK

Makes 1 serving.

1 cup tomato juice, chilled
¼ cup plain yogurt
3 drops Worcestershire sauce
Dash garlic powder
Salt to taste

Whirl all ingredients in container of electric blender just until blended. Serve with cucumber stick.

GRAPE COOLER

Makes 3 servings.

1 cup peach nectar
1 cup white grape juice
1 bottle (8 ounces) carbonated water

Combine peach nectar, grape juice and carbonated water in a pitcher. Stir to mix; pour into ice-filled glasses.

ORANGE JUICE SPARKLER

Makes 1 serving.

¾ cup orange juice
Ice cubes
¼ cup quinine water
Orange slice

Pour orange juice over ice cubes in a glass. Stir in quinine water. Serve with orange slice.

APRICOT-APPLE QUENCHER

Makes 3 servings.

1 can (12 ounces) apricot nectar
1 cup water
½ cup apple juice
Apple wedges

Combine apricot nectar, water and apple juice in small pitcher. Stir to mix. Chill until ready to serve. Pour into 3 tall ice-filled glasses. Garnish with apple wedges.

Beverage

CURRIED CLAM COCKTAIL

Curry and lemon give a fresh flavor lift to this jiffy-fix special.

Makes 4 servings.

- **2 bottles (8 ounces each) clam juice**
- **1 can (8 ounces) tomato sauce**
- **1 tablespoon lemon juice**
- **½ teaspoon curry powder**
- **Crushed ice**

1. Combine clam juice, tomato sauce, lemon juice and curry powder in a 4-cup shaker; shake to mix well.
2. Pour over crushed ice in glasses; serve plain or garnish with a slice of lemon, if you wish.

PIÑA COLADA

Smooth and mellow, one of the big favorites borrowed from the Caribbean.

Makes 2 servings.

- **⅓ cup light rum**
- **½ cup unsweetened pineapple juice**
- **¼ cup cream of coconut (from a 15½-ounce can)**
- **2 tablespoons heavy cream**
- **1 cup crushed ice**
- **Fresh coconut (optional)**
- **Pineapple slices or sticks**
- **Fresh mint sprigs**

Combine rum, pineapple juice, cream of coconut, cream and crushed ice in container of electric blender. Whirl until smooth. Pour over crushed ice in two 10-ounce highball glasses. Or, serve the drinks in a coconut half. Garnish with pineapple and mint; serve with straws.

GUAVA FRUIT PUNCH

Makes 9 cups or 18 four-ounce punch-cup servings.

- **2 cans (7.1 ounces each) guava juice (about 2 cups)**
- **1½ cups unsweetened pineapple juice**
- **1 cup fresh orange juice**
- **¾ cup fresh lemon juice**
- **¼ cup sugar**
- **3 tablespoons grenadine syrup**
- **1 bottle (28 ounces) ginger ale, chilled**
- **Assorted fresh fruit for garnish**

Combine guava, pineapple, orange and lemon juices, sugar and grenadine syrup in 2½-quart container; stir until sugar is dissolved. (Can be prepared ahead to this point.) Just before serving, add ginger ale. Pour over an ice ring in a punch bowl. Garnish individual glasses with skewers of assorted fresh fruit. See **FRUIT KEBABS**, page 64.

PINEAPPLE-MINT COOLER

Sparkling pineapple juice with the cool zip of mint.

Makes about 12 servings.

- **4 cups unsweetened pineapple juice, chilled**
- **½ cup lemon juice**
- **¼ cup green crème de menthe**
- **1 bottle (28 ounces) lemon-lime carbonated beverage**
- **Canned or fresh pineapple slices**

1. Combine pineapple and lemon juices and crème de menthe in a 2½-quart container; mix well. (Can be prepared ahead to this point.)
2. Add carbonated beverage just before serving. Serve over ice cubes in 8-ounce highball glasses; or pour over an ice ring in a punch bowl. Garnish each serving with a quarter pineapple slice.

HAWAIIAN SUNRISE

Makes 1 serving.

- **2 teaspoons grenadine syrup**
- **Ice cubes**
- **¼ cup light rum**
- **1 tablespoon orange-flavored liqueur**
- **¼ cup unsweetened pineapple juice**
- **¼ cup fresh orange juice**
- **2 tablespoons fresh lime juice**
- **1 tablespoon fresh lemon juice**
- **Lemon slice and strawberry**

1. Pour grenadine syrup in bottom of a large, round, footed (about 16-ounce) glass. Fill glass with ice.
2. Combine rum, orange liqueur and pineapple, orange, lime and lemon juices in a small pitcher; mix well. Carefully pour over ice. Stir slightly, if necessary, to give sunrise effect. Garnish with lemon and strawberry.

SCORPION

Very exotic and a great favorite in Polynesian restaurants.

Makes 1 serving.

- **¼ cup dark rum**
- **2 tablespoons brandy**
- **¼ cup fresh orange juice**
- **3 tablespoons fresh lemon juice**
- **1 tablespoon orgeat syrup or amaretto liqueur**
- **1 cup crushed ice**
- **Gardenia**

Combine rum, brandy, orange and lemon juices, orgeat and ice in container of electric blender; whirl 30 seconds. Serve over ice cubes in large footed champagne-type glass. Garnish with gardenia.

MAI TAI

This has many versions throughout the Islands, but is considered the classic Hawaiian drink.

Makes 1 serving.

- **3 tablespoons light rum**
- **2 tablespoons dark rum**
- **1 tablespoon orange-flavored liqueur**
- **1 tablespoon fresh lime juice**
- **1 teaspoon sugar**
- **2 dashes aromatic bitters**
- **Crushed ice**
- **Fresh mint sprigs**

Combine light and dark rums, liqueur, lime juice, sugar and bitters in a cocktail shaker; shake well. Pour over crushed ice in a 6-ounce old-fashioned glass. Or, serve in a scooped out small pineapple. Garnish with mint; serve with straws.

BANANA COW

Creamy and cool — kids will love it!

Makes 2 servings.

- **1 medium-size banana, peeled and cut into chunks**
- **½ cup milk**
- **1 tablespoon honey**
- **⅛ teaspoon vanilla**
- **1 cup crushed ice**
- **Lime wedges**

Combine banana, milk, honey, vanilla and ice in container of electric blender; whirl until smooth. Pour into two 10-ounce highball glasses. Garnish with lime wedges.

Pictured opposite: (From top) Scorpion, Guava Fruit Punch, Mai Tai, Pina Colada, Banana Cow, and Pineapple-Mint Cooler, all page 62

How to Dress Drinks for a Party

Sugar-coated Grapes
Break off dainty bunches and dip into an egg white beaten slightly with about a half teaspoon of water, then into granulated sugar, turning to coat well. Set aside on paper toweling until dry. Drape over rim of a glass.

Citrus Cartwheel
Notch orange and lemon or lime slices around the edge, and thread with a maraschino cherry onto a cocktail or short drinking straw.

Fruit Kebabs
Thread any combination of fruits on drinking straws or stirrer sticks. Make them long or short to fit into a pitcher or glass. Combinations shown here: Watermelon and honeydew balls; cut-up kumquats and chunks of banana rolled in lemon juice and coconut; marshmallows on a candy stick; orange slices and whole strawberries; and raspberries, pear rounds, and blueberries.

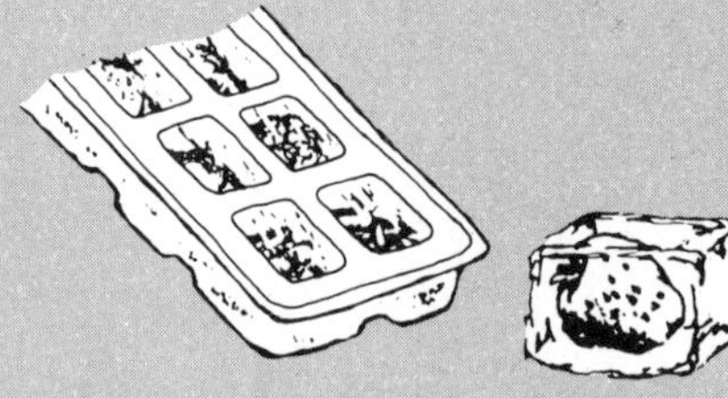

Colorful Cubes
Place a berry; cherry; wedge of orange, lemon, or lime; or a thin strip of peel in each compartment of an ice-cube tray. Fill with water and freeze as usual.

Orange Cup
Just plain, or simply decorated with a sprig of mint, a scooped-out orange makes a colorful cup. Save the fruit to dice and add to salad or dessert.

INDIAN YOGURT DRINK

Makes 1 quart.

1 container (8 ounces) plain yogurt
¼ cup lime juice
3 tablespoons honey
Cold plain or bottled water

1. Put yogurt, lime juice and honey in container of electric blender. Whirl until smooth.
2. Pour into quart container; fill with cold water. Chill; stir before serving.

COCOA

Makes 4 to 6 servings.

3 tablespoons unsweetened cocoa powder
¼ cup sugar
1 quart milk
¼ teaspoon vanilla
4 to 6 marshmallows

1. Blend cocoa and sugar.
2. Heat milk to scalding; mix a little hot milk into cocoa mixture, then add to hot milk and stir until well blended. Add vanilla; pour into cups or mugs and float a marshmallow in each.

CRANBERRY-ORANGE COOLER

Makes 3 servings.

1 cup cranberry juice cocktail
1 cup orange juice
1 cup water
Orange slices

Combine cranberry juice cocktail, orange juice and water in a small pitcher. Stir to mix; chill. Pour into 3 tall ice-filled glasses. Garnish with orange slice.

SUMMERTIME LEMONADE

Nothing like a pitcher of cool homemade lemonade to quench a thirst.

Makes about 2 quarts.

6 cups water
2 cups sugar
2½ cups fresh lemon juice

1. Heat water and sugar to boiling in a medium-size saucepan, stirring constantly. Boil 5 minutes without stirring; cool; chill.
2. Just before serving, combine sugar syrup and lemon juice. Pour over ice in tall glasses. Garnish with strawberries and lemon slices, if you wish.